YOU WILL DO BETTER IN TOLEDO: FROM FROGTOWN TO GLASS CITY

A Toledo Retrospective in Postcards
1893-1929

Edited by
Sandy and John R. Husman

Published by The Blade
September 2008

John Robinson Block
Co-Publisher and Editor-in-Chief, The Blade

Joseph H. Zerbey, IV
Vice President and General Manager

The Blade
541 North Superior Street
Toledo, Ohio 43660
419-724-6545

From the Postcard Collection and Writings of
Ken Levin

Matthew Lentz
Publication Coordinator

Phillip Long
Creative Director/Graphic Designer

Printed in the United States of America by
University Lithoprinters, Ann Arbor, Michigan.

Compact disc produced in the United States of America by
Orange Peel Productions, Inc., Toledo, Ohio.

ISBN: 978-0-9770681-3-5

This book is printed on acid free-paper.

CONTENTS

FOREWORD

The Blade is delighted to introduce a unique history book, **You Will Do Better in Toledo: From Frogtown to Glass City.** Produced with intimate care and a deft touch by knowledgeable editors Sandy and John Husman, it is truly a once-in-a-lifetime collector's item.

This postcard book reveals a portion of our city's history spanning 1880 to 1930, the Golden Age of Toledo. Hundreds of postcards illustrate its pages, nearly all from the collection of Toledoan Ken Levin whose compilation totals more than 3,000. It is much more than a pictorial, however. *You Will Do Better in Toledo* tells the story of Toledo's birth as a prosperous international business community, side-by-side with the birth and evolution of the postcard itself.

One hundred and seventy-six pages showcase authentic black-and-white and full-color reproductions of Levin's original cards. And more than 2,000 cards are included on a searchable compact disc located on the back inside cover. A historical narrative has also been compiled, explaining each postcard's relationship to Toledo's history.

This publication is a labor of love for John and Sandy and a dream come true for Ken whose dearest wish was to share his collection with the people of Northwest Ohio. *The Blade* is pleased and proud to publish it.

Quite simply, it is a work of art, and one that should be in every home with ties to Toledo. I encourage you to follow Ken's selfless example and pass this treasure on to friends and family. What Toledo was, what it became, and what it can yet aspire to be is revealed on its pages.

Make it a part of your library. It is already a part of your history.

Joseph H. Zerbey, IV
Vice President and General Manager

PREFACE

Our initial task as editors of this volume was to act as matchmakers. We brought together Ken Levin, Toledo postcard collector extraordinaire, and *The Blade*, recent publisher of fine Toledo history books. We made a good match.

Ken Levin has been collecting Toledo postcards for 40 years. He has long sought a way to share his comprehensive collection with others. This quality book does that and faithfully reproduces the fine photographs of a century ago. Levin has been involved with this project every step of the way and provided invaluable advice and assistance to the editors. Recognizing that relatively few of his postcards could be included in a book, he suggested the companion searchable compact disc. Levin's objective was to include as many postcards as possible, covering every significant person, building, and event while avoiding unenlightening duplication. He has accomplished that through his selection of postcards and earmarking the best 300 story-telling cards for the book itself.

The Blade began publishing Toledo history books in 2005 when it published the first of the three-volume *Toledo: Our Life, Our Times, Our Town*. This highly successful series featured reader-submitted photographs. *You Will Do Better in Toledo* is a departure from that format but similar in an important way. Once again, *The Blade* is making available to the community an archive of local historical photographs from within the community that otherwise might never have been seen. *The Blade* has made a leap in quality with this all-color coffee table book with its searchable compact disc. The disc contains nearly 2,000 historical postcard photographs and makes this book the first of its kind for Toledo.

Although this began as a picture book, it evolved into a Toledo historical narrative during its making. Like a novel, the book has a story line—a remarkable coincidence. The transformation of Toledo into an urban center with a booming manufacturing-based economy paralleled almost exactly the popularization of the picture postcard. Both events began in the final quarter of the nineteenth century and continued until brought to a halt by the Great Depression. That half century or so was Toledo's finest era. Toledo had been a small crossroads and lake port village but it became a major city. During the same half century, the picture postcard developed as a new media phenomenon for illustrating and preserving almost every major development, accomplishment, and event in the life of the city.

A landmark event, and perhaps the symbol of Toledo's beginning as an industrial giant, was Edward Drummond Libbey's desperate promotion of his struggling Toledo-based glass company at the World's Columbian Exposition in Chicago in 1893. That promotion was a success and not only kept Libbey Glass in business in Toledo, but also started a pattern of attracting other industries to the city and helping it to grow. Coincidentally, that same Chicago World's Fair was also the place where the penny picture postcard was introduced. The postcard and industrial Toledo were born together—in Chicago in 1893. They grew together until 1929. This book shows and tells the story of that growth.

The editors were fortunate to be part of an outstanding team that produced this book. Heading the effort was Joseph H. Zerbey, IV vice president and general manager of *The Blade*. It was his vision that initiated *The Blade's* venture into Toledo history book publishing. It is his continued support that sustains the effort. We appreciate his leadership and *The Blade's* willingness to make this an all-American product.

The editors are indebted to Ken Levin who has generously shared his life's endeavor and his time to make this book possible. We also appreciate the contributions of Ken's former associate deltiologists, Jim Black and William Gerwin. Levin considers himself the guardian of the postcard collection and has unselfishly made it available to all. He is also a knowledgeable local historian who put his knowledge to good use on this project. Levin provided the basic outline and nearly all of the initial writing for the volume.

The staff at *The Blade* was responsible for putting the book together. Project Manager Matt Lentz was just that and did an outstanding job of coordinating the graphics, sales, marketing, and advertising functions. As you leaf through this book, your eyes are feasting on the work of Creative Director/Graphic Designer Phillip Long. He is a remarkable artist, loaded with creative ideas, and made this part of the book's work a pleasure for us. Kelly Norwood of *The Blade's* Marketing Department is on board with her vast knowledge of the Toledo market. Her real work begins after the book is completed and ready for sale.

Levin's collection of Toledo historical postcards is exhaustive but not complete. No collection ever could be, as many cards are lost forever and others, currently unknown, could surface at any time. Even though his collection is the most inclusive in existence and will never be duplicated, he has sought out some additional postcards for this book. The following have contributed postcards to help make this volume as comprehensive and inclusive as possible: Larry Boltz, Charlene Dane, James K. Drewyor, Fred Folger, Gary Gatanis, Tom Helmke, Lynn Menke, Harry Schroeder, Mark Walczak, Toledo-Lucas County Public Library, and *The Blade*.

We also wish to thank our proofreaders and fact-checkers. All have helped us by doing a critical job with objective honesty. Our daughter, Marianne Quellhorst, may have had the most difficult job of all—the first read. Virtually all of her countless suggestions have been incorporated into the work. Fred Folger, the preeminent Toledo historian, brought suggestions that could only come from him. His intimate knowledge of Toledo's history is unmatched. We rest easy with the facts presented here because of his approval. Thanks are also due to our proofreaders, Kim Brownlee, Jim Marshall, and Denise Meyer. They were not only thorough in their task, but quick about it.

Much of the information utilized in the narrative and descriptions throughout this book was uncovered in the course of many hours spent working with the vast resources found in the collections of the Local History and Genealogy Department of the Toledo-Lucas County Public Library. The encyclopedic knowledge, dogged persistence in tracking down obscure data, and unfailing courtesy and helpfulness of the entire staff has contributed significantly to the content and quality of this book. We thank Manager Mike Lora, Donna Christian, Ann Hurley, Irene Martin, Greg Miller, and Laura Voelz.

Research assistance was also provided by Kim Brownlee at The Ward M. Canaday Center, The University of Toledo Libraries and Julie McMaster, archivist, the Toledo Museum of Art.

Many other individuals have helped—some in substantial ways, some in smaller ways. Taken in total their contributions are significant. Our thanks to Hanady Awada, Tim Boaden, Sue Brickey, Nancy Bucher, John Crisp, Bonnie Dickson, Ken Dickson, Margarita Duran, Barbara Floyd, Pam Griesinger, Jordie Henry, Lou Hibbs, Tina Hibbs, Kim Johns, Pam Kantola, John Lane, Michelle Lane, Bob Levin, Ron Mauter, Jim Meyers, Larry Michaels, Greg Ogrodowski, Steve Quellhorst, Tammy Reagan, Sandra Reams, Ron Royhab, Isabel Sloan, April Spangler, Tom Sutherland, Harry Villalon, Mark Walczak, Melinda Walczak and Sara Welborn.

Ryan Mininger of Orange Peel Productions provided scanning and formatting services as well as much-needed direction for the digital aspects of the project. Carrie Dennison of University Lithoprinters deftly guided us through the intricacies of the book printing business.

The editors have learned a great deal about postcards and the history of Toledo while assembling *You Will Do Better in Toledo*. We know what a great, productive, and glorious city Toledo was a century ago. Our hope is that Toledoans will recognize this and strive to rekindle our former positive spirit and move forward into a new "Positive Era". We did it before and we can do it again.

Thank you again to Ken Levin and *The Blade*.

Sandy and John R. Husman

COLLECTOR'S NOTES

If a picture really is worth a thousand words, this may be one of the longest books ever produced. This book and companion compact disc include an archive of nearly 2,000 postcards. The book's main purpose is to demonstrate how—a century ago, for only a penny—the humble picture postcard not only created a revolution in communications, but also left a marvelously complete history of Toledo's finest era—the half century from around 1880 to 1930. The city was transformed from an ordinary Midwestern lake port town into a modern, manufacturing-based urban center with that distinctive identity we recognize as Toledo.

Most of the 2,000 postcard images included in the book and compact disc are from a collection assembled during a forty-year collaborative effort by life-long Toledo residents, the late William Gerwin and Ken Levin. Over the years, dozens of people have helped by finding and providing cards for the collection. The late Jim Black, originally of Monclova Township, deserves special acknowledgement. He not only diligently pursued and acquired rare and valuable items for the collection, but also gave sound, practical advice on what developments and events in Toledo's past deserve remembering. His unfailing optimism and drive—despite a 30-year struggle with debilitating multiple sclerosis—was inspirational. He constantly prodded and encouraged that the collection be made available to everyone. Without his encouragement this book may never have come to fruition.

To aid users in locating specific pictures or subjects in this large and fascinating body of historical images, the following explanation of how the material is arranged may be helpful. Since the subject matter is concentrated in a specific era, chronological arrangement is not so critical as to preclude arranging the chapters by topics, illustrated with representative sample views. The main advantage of such a topical approach is that the user is free to browse the book without worrying about the overall context. Secondly, knowing the subject in question was pictured on postcards prompts the user to look for other related images on the compact disc. To ease accessibility to the electronic images, a user-friendly index has been included on the compact disc. Cross references to topics, categories, names, and key words will help the viewer search for related items. Instructions, suggestions, and prompts to help the viewer in these searches are explained on the compact disc.

The chapters are arranged so that readers, who start at the beginning and work their way through the book, should have an opportunity to gradually become aware of a bigger overall picture. They will recognize major factors, forces, and dynamics behind the way a modern city developed. The huge number and variety of pictures should help develop an appreciation of the extraordinary richness of the activities and events that have become Toledo's legacy. That much can be learned is largely because so many postcards were produced during the time period. They allow us to develop an overall understanding of the city's heritage.

Chapter 1 recounts the technological advances that led to the rise of postcards, and explains how they left a huge illustrated record of the rise of the City of Toledo during its second half century. Chapter 2 provides the background for that rise during the city's first fifty years. It shows how accidents of location made Toledo a crossroads hub, leading much of its development and economic livelihood naturally toward shipping, distribution, and all the forms of transportation needed to move goods and people. Chapters 3 and 4 tell how the arrival of industries, especially glass, toward the end of the nineteenth century and automobiles at the beginning of the twentieth century, changed the entire economic base. They accelerated growth and transformed the city. Chapters 5 and 6 describe the physical development of the new metropolis. Chapter 5 concentrates on the rise of business and commercial facilities, retail stores, and wholesale supply networks. Chapter 6 covers the development of monumental architecture in skyscrapers, public and institutional buildings, and new residential neighborhoods. Chapter 7 discusses domestic, social, and political matters. It includes ways the city provided basic utilities and services, the development of modern conveniences, acquisition of land for parks, and the political reforms of the Progressive Era. Chapter 8 covers the development of institutions and facilities for leisure, recreation, sports, entertainment, theater, culture, and the arts. Chapters 9 and 10 are devoted to a selected number of specific developments and events that were considered important or interesting enough to be the subjects of numerous postcards.

One of the fascinating sidelights of studying history is the chance to compare the situations and conditions faced by earlier generations with similar issues at the present time. The current population has the same concerns about productive jobs, earning a living, and enjoying a good quality of life. The most basic conditions and problems keep presenting themselves from one era to the next. As readers of the book follow the way Toledoans tackled problems during the city's first century, reflection on what worked and what did not, as well as what conditions are different now, could very well give rise to ways of keeping Toledo on the move in the twenty-first century. The city's very future could depend on making good decisions, and understanding what was done in the past can only help.

Ken Levin

CHAPTER ONE
THE PICTURE POSTCARD AND THE TOLEDO COINCIDENCE

During the summer of 1893, the United States was embroiled in economic panic and about to enter a depression. The boom in economic development that had prevailed since the Civil War had markedly slowed and the great optimistic attitude about the country's future had dampened.

The economy was so bleak that two Toledo businessmen, cousins Adelbert L. and Celian M. Spitzer, were forced to stop construction on their new high-rise office building at the corner of Madison Avenue[1] and Huron Street. At ten stories, it was to be Toledo's biggest and first truly modern skyscraper as well as the first with a steel frame. The structure was already coming out of the ground when Adelbert Spitzer traveled to Pittsburgh to beg Andrew Carnegie to void their contract for the building's steel. Carnegie granted the request and the Spitzers paid for the portion of steel already delivered. Consequently, the Spitzer Building site sat idle surrounded by a wooden fence for some time thereafter. The Spitzer edifice was finally completed and opened in 1896.

Another Toledo businessman, Edward Drummond Libbey, was also struggling. Despite many incentives given by the Toledo community, his Libbey Glass Company plant had not been profitable since he brought it to Toledo from New England in 1888. He decided to gamble the company's future by spending a small fortune to develop a working model of a glass factory for the great World's Columbian Exposition, better known as the Chicago World's Fair of 1893. His exhibit and samples of fine glass products were a success and orders soon began flooding into his factory from all over the country and other parts of the world. Moreover, Libbey's success was a pivotal event for Toledo as it promoted the advantages of the city to outsiders and led several major businesses to relocate there. The city thus embarked on a new course of growth and development. It was transformed from a small river and lake

Spitzer Bldg., Toledo, O.

SPITZER BUILDING

1. Madison Avenue was Madison Street before 1902.

port village into a modern twentieth-century urban center with a manufacturing base. The transformation began with the success of The Libbey Glass Company and continued at a rapid and sustained pace until the Great Depression began in 1929. It was the most important and productive era in Toledo's history. This era, from the mid-1890s until 1929, gave the city its own identity and its distinctive character.

LIBBEY GLASS FACTORY

Also at the Chicago World's Fair, the penny picture postal card was introduced by the United States Postal Service. The Postal Service had been the exclusive supplier of postal cards or postals[2] since they began issuing the pre-stamped cards in 1873. Like previously issued government postals, the address side was already imprinted with a one-cent postage stamp and the words "The United States of America." The opposite side was blank for the user's written message. The innovation of the Chicago World's Fair postals over plain government cards was that the front side of the souvenir cards contained colorful renderings of buildings and scenes from the Fair along with the official seal of the Exposition. Visitors could purchase these cards at various places around the grounds—even from vending machines, write a short message on some white space

2. In 1893, postals were government issued and preprinted with one-cent postage. Any other cards or letters that were privately issued required a two-cent stamp.

intentionally left on the picture side, and then drop the card into a mailbox. The Chicago World's Fair cards were official souvenirs.

COLUMBIAN EXPOSITION

A remarkable coincidence occurred at the Chicago World's Fair of 1893 that would not be realized until it played out years later. The Fair that helped jump start Libbey and put Toledo on its fast track of development also began the popularization of the postcard. Toledo and the postcard industry shared a common nativity and grew together, complementing each other's growth. The development of Toledo was documented by thousands of picture postcards of Toledo scenes that were made over the next three decades.

These illustrated souvenir postals proved to be a great idea whose time had come. They became so popular that they created a veritable revolution in communications which swept the country.

To realize the excitement of sending pictures through the mail, one has only to think about how people communicated in the last quarter of the nineteenth century. Electricity had indeed been discovered and the telephone was invented in 1876, but all communication via these media had to be over wires. In Toledo, fewer than ten percent of homes even had a telephone. Photography had advanced since its introduction in the mid-nineteenth century but producing a picture was still a time-consuming and costly process. It required expensive and bulky equipment as well as processing skills. Taking pictures was therefore left mostly in the hands of a few professionals. Because of the time, labor, and cost involved, most newspapers and periodicals did not publish pictures. Even if one could obtain a photograph, sending it through the mail was relatively expensive. With the exception of the government-issued postal cards, any standard letter or card cost the sender two cents. Thus, the ability to send pictures conveniently through the mail for only a penny captured the public's imagination. In addition, the business community saw a huge advertising potential in the picture postcard and clamored for a penny rate for privately produced cards. Congress approved the Private Mailing Card Act on May 19, 1898, permitting the penny rate for "private mailing cards." The stage was set for explosive growth of the postcard industry.

The halving of the postage rate opened huge new commercial marketing opportunities. Professional photographers immediately began producing picture cards on all types of subjects—holiday greetings, art, portraits, people and events, and all kinds of local views such as street scenes, buildings, monuments, historical sites, schools, churches, parks, homes, factories, businesses, boats, trains, trolleys, river and lake scenes, and any other scene likely to attract a buyer. Inevitably, several large companies emerged as leaders and producers of these views. They sent photographers across the country, and began to flood the market with views of popular local sites.

Perhaps the best of these large American firms was the Detroit Publishing Company, which obtained exclusive rights to an advanced printing process that allowed them to mechanically add bright colors to the black and white prints of the day. Between 1895 and 1924, they produced over 16,000 different views, including several different series of Toledo cards that included this scene at Toledo's popular Walbridge Park.

Even bigger was the Rotograph Company. With offices in New York and Chicago, it produced over 60,000 different high-quality cards, including many of the best early pictorial representations of Toledo taken just after the turn of the century. Here, in 1905, one of their products captures their own cameraman photographing homes in Bronson Place, one of Toledo's upscale new subdivisions and one of the city's first "gated" communities.

BRONSON PLACE

Rotograph and many other publishers in the business relied heavily on European producers for coloring and lithographing services. Their more highly-developed technology and sophisticated production equipment, particularly in Germany and Italy, were

WALBRIDGE PARK

superior to most of their counterparts in the United States. To compare Europe's and America's best products, see Rotograph's following image of the same Walbridge Park scene as that of the Detroit Publishing Company shown on the previous page. Both have good points, but one critical consideration was that Rotograph could have its cards made in Germany at less cost.

Pythian Castle. Toledo, Ohio

PYTHIAN CASTLE

THE REIDHOLD OPITZ FOUNTAIN WALBRIDGE PARK TOLEDO, O.

WALBRIDGE PARK

The superiority of European technology and manufacturing in producing the popular new postcards led the Europeans to take advantage of a growing business opportunity in the vast market of burgeoning America. The German manufacturers in particular sent agents to the United States to set up offices and develop sales and distribution networks. This linked the German card makers directly to local retailers like stationers, book sellers, drug stores, and department stores who wished to offer their own brand of views for sale. In this way, the European manufacturers were able to eliminate the American producer and printed the local business name on the card as the "publisher." Both of the following two cards—the first showing the Pythian Castle and Burt's Theater on Jefferson Avenue and the second a view west on Monroe Street in downtown Toledo— were commissioned and published this way by Milner's, Toledo's largest department store of the time.

Monroe Street. Toledo, Ohio.

MONROE STREET

Superior Street, South from Adams, Toledo, Ohio.

SUPERIOR STREET

The view south on Superior Street from Adams Street was produced for and "published" exclusively by the S.H. Knox Company, another major downtown retail store. Other businesses also published cards. *The Toledo Blade*, already over 70 years old in 1906, issued several sets of black and white souvenir postcards of

A Bunch of Blade Hustlers, Toledo, O.

BLADE HUSTLERS

scenes and events around Toledo. *The Blade* cards numbered 32 in all including this one showing a group of their younger workers.

As the twentieth century began, racks in almost every retail store and newsstand were loaded with local view cards and sales exploded. Obviously, one of the keys to this growth was that the new medium was—and had to remain—affordable. The Postal Service had done its part by halving the standard mailing rate to a penny. The cost of the card itself was the other half of the equation. Delivering a finished card to a retail seller required a number of steps beginning with obtaining a traveling photographer to capture local views popular enough to attract a buyer. After the image was developed, every part of the black and white negative was coded so a technician could color each detail properly. Generally, the negatives and information were then sent—by ship—to a European production facility for printing. The finished product was returned across the Atlantic, and delivered to the American retailer. One has to marvel that the business could be profitable at all. Cost of production was a major part of the reason that it was. Typically, the wholesale cost to a retailer from a German manufacturer for one thousand postcards of the same view, including shipping, was about six dollars.

In the early years of the century, retailers sold postcards for two or three cents apiece. As competition and the number of offerings grew, prices began to drop to a point where a retail price of one cent became common. Some sellers even began offering six for a nickel. In 1912, F.W. Woolworth set out millions of cards in its chain stores across the country at ten cents per dozen. Calculating from this cost and pricing data, retailers were probably achieving a profit of about one-third cent per card. The purchasing power of a penny at the beginning of the twentieth century compares roughly to today's quarter. Using that relationship, mailing a letter at two cents and a postcard at one cent a century ago would be roughly the same as mailing a letter at fifty cents and a postcard at twenty-five cents today. Also, a profit of one-third cent per card sold a century ago would translate into an equivalent profit today of about eight cents per card. The Postal Service delivered 900 million postcards in 1913. Since a large percentage of cards, probably even more one hundred years ago than today, is purchased as souvenirs and never mailed, it is likely that at least a billion postcards were purchased in 1913. This made the humble penny postcard, in terms of current dollars, a $250 million a year business.

With that kind of money involved, it is not difficult to understand why the postcard business grew. In addition to the establishment of the large postcard-producing companies, many individuals with photographic expertise and equipment began taking advantage of this popular new medium to produce local views as well as studio portraits and family pictures printed on postcard backs. One of the best of these professional individuals was Louis James Pesha. A Canadian, he moved to Marine City, Michigan, and opened a photographic studio in 1901. Pesha soon became recognized for producing high-quality photographs of the commercial lake boats that sailed by his studio. Many of them were printed as postcards. Traveling around Michigan and down into northern Ohio, he took pictures of many local scenes. His postcards were perhaps of the highest technical excellence at that time. He photographed over one hundred views, including the following sharp 1910 scene of children playing in the water at Toledo's City Park (now Rev. H.V. Savage Park).

Pesha's photos and especially his postcards are considered among the finest ever produced. His work is still widely and avidly collected nearly a century later.

Several native Toledo professionals also produced photo postcards. Edward M. Wright nearly matched Pesha in the technical quality of his local scenes. His studio at 221 Summit Street near Jefferson Avenue, in the heart of Toledo's busiest commercial district, is featured on one of his own street view postcards.

SUMMIT STREET

CITY PARK

CHILDREN AND GOAT CART

The most prolific local postcard photographer and producer was Louis A. Bush, who established the L.A. Bush Photo Postcard Company around 1905. On the previous marvelous card showing children at play, the boy in the goat cart is identified as Richard Harrison. As the camera sharply reveals, Harrison is the object of an astonishingly wide range of emotions—curiosity, mirth, anxiety, envy and even rapt attention from the dog. The back of the card advertises "Souvenir Postcards, L.A. Bush, Commercial Photographer, 710 Redwood Avenue, Toledo, Ohio."

The idea that portraits and posed family photos could be mailed to family and friends for a penny was also a popular way to use postcards. Retailers such as department stores, interurban and train stations, and many other businesses set up their own in-house portrait studios. There, an almost "instant" portrait could be taken, developed and printed on a postcard while the customer waited or—even better—occupied time shopping in the store. For example, in 1910, W. L. Milner's in-store studio made this photo postcard of two well-dressed Toledo children.

BOY AND GIRL

TOLEDO NEWSBOYS' BAND

The image on the preceeding page of two members of the Toledo Newsboys' Band posing with their instruments was also taken at Milner's.

As the following example shows, Tiedtke's Department Store offered customers cut-out silhouette caricatures of themselves pasted on a postcard as souvenir novelties.

Studio portraits were also produced by individual photographers, including Toledo's Elmer Whitney in his Whitney Studio at 715 Cherry Street. Whitney also found creative ways to make use of postcards to advertise, taking advantage of the postcard's ability to communicate quickly and easily. This 1911 postcard features a self-portrait, to be used as something similar to a business card. It also served as a sample for the customer of the kind of work he could do. In the message on the back, the photographer explains to his customer, Mrs. Mollie Binkley, that her baby moved when having its portrait made. He asks her to return to have the photo retaken.

SILHOUETTE

ELMER WHITNEY

The message also demonstrates how the postcard became the primary medium of communication over distance. This came about because the Postal Service delivered mail quickly. In Toledo mail was delivered twice a day. Several postcards exist which state, "I'll be home today." In this example, Whitney asks his customer if she can return that same afternoon.

In Toledo, in the early years of the twentieth century, it was convenient and inexpensive to acquire picture postcards from almost anywhere and depicting almost any topic imaginable. In the following postcard from one hundred years ago, note the display rack featuring some of the postcards featured in this book. The site of this newsstand was in the lobby of the Jefferson Hotel located at the corner of Jefferson Avenue and St. Clair Street.

JEFFERSON HOTEL NEWSSTAND

Hundreds of millions of this fast, new form of communication were turned out annually by everyone from huge producers to individual photographers in their own home studios. A postcard album became a fixture in almost every home.

One factor which contributed to the development of postcards was the means for the general public to make their own cards.

This was provided by George Eastman who in the late 1880s perfected flexible rolled film and a lightweight portable box camera that was simple enough to be operated by almost anyone. These inventions allowed the photographer to dispense with heavy equipment and cumbersome glass negatives. In 1900, the Eastman Kodak Company[3] introduced the "Brownie" box camera which sold for $1.00. A roll of film with enough room for six to ten exposures cost fifteen cents. Then in 1903 Kodak issued the "Folding Pocket Camera" which was more compact and produced better pictures from negatives that were the exact size of postcards. Now everyone—even those with no experience in photography at all—could make their own pictures. George Eastman's plan was to provide the public with a simple method of making pictures. The Kodak early advertising slogan was, "You press the button, we do the rest." He believed that young people would be the first to embrace the new technology. Promotion and even naming the "Brownie" camera were aimed at the youngest consumers. His final goal was speed—he wanted to take advantage of people's desire to communicate with others as quickly as possible. Kodak could develop the film for customers, but that took time. So the company soon began providing the equipment and chemicals needed to set up simple darkrooms in homes. This allowed the public, not only to develop their own pictures, but also to print them directly on Kodak's new photo paper. The thicker paper was already cut to postcard size with the emulsion pre-coated on one side and the words "Post Card" with a postage stamp box pre-printed on the back. Now anyone could take a picture, develop it at home, print it directly onto a postcard, affix a stamp, and mail it—all within a matter of hours. In comparison, the result was a quantum leap in the speed of communication. The general public, particularly young people, embraced it with great enthusiasm. The following postcard features a photograph of Alice Curtiss, who was born in Toledo in 1892 and lived in the city all her life.[4] Like many others, she purchased one of the new Kodak cameras as a teenager and took

3. The original Eastman Company became Eastman Kodak in 1892 and is commonly referred to as Kodak. The Kodak name was devised by Eastman himself. The letter k was a favorite of his. He tried various combinations of letters to form a word starting and ending in k before settling on Kodak.

4. Alice Curtiss was a grandmother of Ken Levin, the deltiologist whose collection is featured in this book.

many pictures of family and friends, including this self-portrait. She developed it herself and printed it on Kodak's postcard developing paper to send to her friends.

ALICE CURTISS

Thousands of other people around the country did the same. To gauge the impact of this phenomenon on public behavior, one might compare the effect of similar more recent leaps in communications technology, such as the cellular telephone.

The advances in photography that allowed anyone to take pictures were also responsible for the existence of many of the rarest and best images we now have. They chronicle what life was like and remind us of events in our past which might otherwise be forgotten.

One obstacle to communication via the new postcard medium was the limited space available for text or a written message. Since the United States Postal Service required that any message be written on the picture side of the card, some blank area had to be left, diminishing the size of the picture. Moreover, writing on photo paper that had been treated with developing emulsion proved difficult. The Eastman Kodak Company did address this latter problem by including a pointed metal stylus with its postcard-developing paper so the printer could scratch a short description right on to the negative. The words then appear as white on the printed photo. In 1907 the Postal Service finally responded to complaints of limited message space by allowing the back side to be divided, with the address and stamp on the right half and any messages or text on the left. From then on the photograph could cover the entire front of the card, and the quality and even the artistic merit of the photography noticeably improved.

The years between 1907 and World War I (1914-1918) were thus the true high point of the picture postcard. Collectors, or deltiologists, call this era "The Golden Age." In those years, Americans bought more than a billion postcards annually. The postcard was the fastest, least expensive and most effective way available to communicate. However, change is inevitable. In the case of the postcard, the huge economic benefits of the business, with some of the profits going to foreign suppliers, led eventually to the imposition of restrictive tariffs on their importation.[5] This resulted in upward force on costs and prices. The World War then devastated Europe, which made the tariffs irrelevant when many of the plants producing postcards were destroyed. Forced to absorb the resulting increased costs and the use of inferior printing equipment and technology, American printers and publishers began to cut back drastically on the types and number of cards produced. Other cost-cutting measures were employed such as reducing ink usage by increasing the size of the border on the card. Quality suffered and the "The Golden Age" came to an end almost overnight. New printing processes also allowed newspapers and magazines

5. The Payne-Aldrich Tariff Act of 1909 effectively cut off low-cost importation of postcards, along with many other goods.

to increasingly publish pictures, thereby reducing the need to use postcards to send visual news. By the 1920s, the automobile shortened travel time, and made it easier to communicate in person. And perhaps the biggest change was the ever-increasing availability and use of the telephone, which made instant communication by voice much easier. The beginnings of radio broadcasting, which took place right in downtown Toledo, were rendering obsolete the old methods of communication. Remnants of the postcard business limped on into the twenties. The communications phenomenon had begun in Chicago at the start of a depression in 1893. Ironically, the economic collapse of 1929 and the beginning of the Great Depression brought an effective end to the importance of the postcard.

The period of Toledo's greatest growth and the shaping and development of its distinctive identity also took place in those same years between the depressions. It began with Edward Drummond Libbey's success at the Chicago World's Fair of 1893, and grew at a spectacular pace until the Crash of 1929 brought it to a sudden and devastating halt.

By this very coincidence, we have a marvelous illustrated record of the rise and development of Toledo in what was undoubtedly its finest hour. The humble penny postcards chronicled and documented a positive and inspiring story. Toledoans, who were creating a great city and a good life, optimistically and proudly proclaimed, "You Will Do Better in Toledo."

The Toledoan's Creed was published in 1913 by the Toledo Commerce Club—a precursor of today's Toledo Regional Chamber of Commerce.

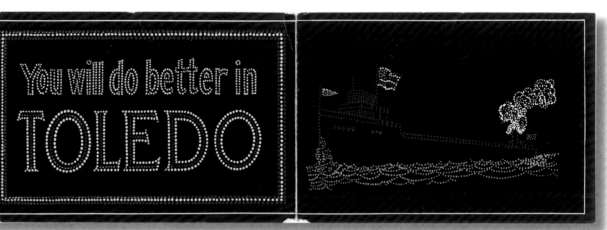

YOU WILL DO BETTER IN TOLEDO
——— WHY? ———

BECAUSE:

Unsurpassed transportation facilities.
34 steam and electric roads and several steamship lines.
Superior for distribution—a natural manufacturing and jobbing center.
Toledo Terminal Railroad—32 miles long—encircles the city, connecting all railroads and factories.
A great market, near the center of population.
Within one night's ride of 50 million people—one-half the population of the United States.
One of the LARGEST and BEST HARBORS on the Great Lakes.
Excels all other ports in shipments of soft coal by water.

BECAUSE:

Low rates for electrical power.
Fuel at low prices.
A school system of more than an average efficiency—two of the finest High Schools in the country just completed and more to follow at once.
Low rents.
Favorable labor conditions.
A city of homes—active, aggressive and progressive.
A good city in which to live and in which to make a living.
19 large banks.
Population 200,000.

For further information, address   THE TOLEDO COMMERCE CLUB, Toledo, Ohio

𝕻ost 𝕮ard.

10⁰⁰

PLACE
ONE CENT
STAMP
HERE

SALIENT FACTS ABOUT TOLEDO'S SLOGAN SIGN

78 feet long, 68 feet high, weighs 25 tons.   Lighted by 7,000 10 watt Mazda lamps.
Only sign so far constructed with 3 massive moving signs on one frame.   Largest municipal Electric slogan sign ever built.
Was presented to the city by the Toledo Railways & Light Company through The Toledo Commerce Club.

Toledo's slogan sign was presented to the city through the Toledo Commerce Club by the Toledo Railways & Light Company. The slogan itself was chosen from more than 7,000 entries submitted in a contest sponsored by the Toledo Commerce Club. Located atop the Valentine Building at Adams and St. Clair streets, the sign alternated between three images with its 7,000 ten-watt electric lights—the slogan, a railroad locomotive, and a lake freighter. Though this postcard states the sign's dimensions were 78 feet by 68 feet, its appearance and other sources suggest that it was 100 feet by 58 feet. It was reported to weigh 25 tons. The sign was accepted by Mayor Brand Whitlock and first lit on December 17, 1913. According to The Toledo Blade from the following day, "8,000 spectators jammed into St. Clair St., between Madison Ave. and Adams St. to view the sign." The sign remained until 1926 when the City of Toledo offices moved from the Valentine Building to the Safety Building.

CHAPTER TWO

FROGTOWN IN THE NINETEENTH CENTURY

Accidents of location and geography placed Toledo on an important crossroad that became the basis for its economic development during the first three quarters of the nineteenth century. During those years the city became an important hub for shipping and distribution, utilizing all the major transport forms of the time. The city's economic base centered on commerce related to moving people and goods.

In 1800 approximately 90 percent of the country's population lived east of the Allegheny Mountains. Thomas Jefferson became the country's third president in 1801. Ohio became the nation's seventeenth state in 1803. The area that was to become Toledo was an undeveloped wilderness of forests, marshes, and swampland. Because of its strategic location, many early travelers—in their relentless drive into the heartland—found their way to and through Toledo. In just 50 years settlement of Middle America became so extensive that Toledo's position changed. It was then east of the country's population center. At the century's midpoint, steam-powered boats plied the Great Lakes, a network of canals through Ohio and Indiana had been built, and railroad lines established. Major transportation networks were concentrated in and around Toledo. Shipping and transportation services created new jobs and brought a huge amount of business to the area, attracting entrepreneurs and laborers alike. In contrast, for most of the nineteenth century, local industries and manufacturing remained meager. Even into the 1870s, the biggest local industries were brewing beer, roasting and packaging coffee beans, and processing tobacco and lumber.

By the end of the Civil War, Toledo's population had increased to over 20,000, making Toledo a "city of the first class" by terms of the Constitution of the State of Ohio. This classification allowed the city to establish a metropolitan police force, fire-fighting companies, and other essential municipal services. By the 1870s sewers had been installed, draining the swamps from the city center. A public water

pumping plant had been established along the Maumee River at the south edge of town, greatly improving sanitation and overall living conditions. Two- and three-story commercial buildings appeared along Summit Street between Monroe and Cherry streets. Also in the 1870s a larger scale of building began a block to the west on St. Clair Street. A spectacular five-story, 150-room hotel opened at Madison Avenue and St. Clair Street in 1872. The Boody House, one of the finest and most modern structures of its type, was the first building known and talked about outside Toledo. The Hall Block, another five-story building, followed in 1875. This multi-tenant trade mart complemented the hotel and filled almost the rest of the St. Clair Street block to Jefferson Avenue.

Old photographs show how much commerce depended on the shipping of raw materials and agricultural products. The banks of Swan Creek at the south end of town were piled high with lumber from the forests of Ohio and Michigan. So much corn and other grain found its way through Toledo by rail and boat that a dozen large elevators were built on the riverbanks. Local businessmen envisioned the city becoming the central grain broker for the whole country. In 1876 a group of them established the Produce Exchange, a trading house for buying and selling futures in grain. The enterprise was so successful that the Exchange built its own five-story building at Madison Avenue and St. Clair Street in 1878. Through the 1880s the grain shipping business in Toledo grew. Eventually cities in closer proximity to the heart of the grain-growing region of the Great Plains garnered much of the trade, leaving Toledo as a secondary player in that area.

In 1875 the city lured its first major manufacturer—the Milburn Wagon Company, one of the largest providers of transportation products in the country. However, most of the local business continued to revolve predominantly around transport and shipping. When picture postcards began to appear around the turn of the twentieth century, many of them proudly depicted transport or shipping-related accomplishments of the 1870s as the main source of Toledo's growth and prosperity.

After the Civil War, optimism for Toledo's role as a great potential hub of commerce was running high. At that time, Jessup W. Scott, one of the city's pioneer entrepreneurs, wrote a treatise predicting that Toledo's perfect central location and easy access to all of the country's resources would someday make it "the future great city of the world." By 1880 there was little reason to doubt that it might be so. The population had soared past 50,000, and Toledo's durability as a transportation and shipping center seemed certain.

The pioneers who first settled along the Maumee River found overcoming the physical and environmental conditions difficult and often frustrating. One of the difficulties was the huge frog population that afflicted downtown Toledo. In 1838, a year after the city was incorporated, a severe drought temporarily dried up the swampy pools covering most of the downtown west of Summit Street. In plague-like numbers, the frogs were forced to seek water by migrating to the Maumee River. Summit Street was said to be so covered by the desperate amphibians that the approximately 3,000 human residents in town could hardly take a single step without squashing one. Toledo soon became known far and wide as "Frogtown." Long after the downtown swamp was drained and a city grew in its place, the "Toledo Frog" remained an icon symbolizing the city's beginnings.

View of Maumee River, Above City, Toledo, Ohio.

MAUMEE RIVER

Northwestern Ohio's most outstanding geographical feature, the Maumee River is the largest waterway draining into the Great Lakes. The river was a major source of Toledo's livelihood. The city grew hugging the Maumee on both sides and used the rich resource for commerce, industry, recreation, and many of the needs of daily life. Flowing close to 150 miles from Fort Wayne, it actually ends near the city of Perrysburg after a series of rapids. It then flows across a limestone bar into a deeper and wider extension of Maumee Bay with Lake Erie reaching to meet it. From that point on it is an estuary, meaning that for its final fifteen miles or so, its water level fluctuates with that of Lake Erie. In the early days, the spot just above where the river and bay met became significant as the limestone bar was the first place upriver shallow enough for people to ford. For Toledo to succeed, it was important to find a way to cross the Maumee.

12653 WATER FRONT, TOLEDO, OHIO.

TOLEDO'S RIVER BRIDGE

In 1865 a private contractor built and maintained Toledo's first river bridge at the foot of Cherry Street. Tolls were charged to cross the lengthy wooden span. This situation was particularly irritating to residents of the East Side, so the city finally bought the bridge in 1872 and opened it to all traffic at no charge. Maintenance costs for the wooden structure soon became onerous for the taxpayers. Finally, in 1883, the worst spring flood on record damaged the bridge so badly it had to be replaced with the steel swing bridge shown on this postcard. This picture, taken from the East Side circa 1906, shows part of the waterfront of the old Vistula section of the city. The tall steeple at the far left is St. Mary's (German) Catholic Church on Cherry Street. The dark, square cupola just below the steeple is St. Francis de Sales Catholic Church.

CHERR ST BRIDGE TOLEDO OHIO

CHERRY STREET BRIDGE

The Cherry Street Bridge was the main crossing between downtown Toledo and the East Side. Both trolleys and interurban cars carried large numbers of people across in the days before the automobile. The bridge was also a critical lifeline for essential services. It carried lines that provided electricity to the entire East Side until 1918. In 1908 when the steamer Yuma wrecked part of the bridge*, the 25,000 residents of the East Side lived without electricity until a temporary span could be hastily constructed. At that point the city realized a new stronger bridge was needed.

* For more information about the *Yuma* incident, see Chapter 10.

NEW CHERRY STREET BRIDGE

ICE JAM.   MAUMEE RIVER, TOLEDO, O.

9827

MAUMEE RIVER ICE JAM

The new bridge—a bascule (draw) rather than a swing type—was made of concrete and steel. It took over three years to complete, finally opening in 1913. By the time it was finished, costs nearly doubled the original estimate which forced the city to eliminate four ornate towers planned to give the bridge a distinct and more imposing appearance. The "new" Cherry Street Bridge* has served Toledo for nearly a century.

* The Cherry Street Bridge was renamed the Dr. Martin Luther King, Jr. Bridge on January 12, 1988. Since the bridge was the Cherry Street Bridge during the time frame of this book, the name will be used hereinafter.

NO.69. WATER ST FOOT OF MADISON FLOODED. 3-6-08. TOLEDO. O.

WATER STREET FLOOD

Even though bridges made crossing easier, the Maumee River was still a mighty force of nature. Flooding, caused by blocking ice jams in February and March, was a threat almost every year. Fortunately for Toledo, the river becomes wider and deeper as it flows to the lake, sparing the city from some of the worst flooding that plagues upriver towns. Nevertheless, Toledo has not been entirely free of flooding as illustrated on this 1908 postcard showing people wading on Water Street.

GRAIN ELEVATOR "B"

COAL DOCKS

IRON ORE DOCKS

The main benefit of living along the Maumee River was the livelihood it provided as a liquid highway for commerce and industry. Toledo's early business centered on shipping and transportation. Agricultural products and natural resources, such as lumber, from the region could be shipped both east and west via the Great Lakes. By the end of the nineteenth century, Toledo had at least twelve large grain elevators. These were located on both the east (shown here) and west sides of the river, on the Middlegrounds near the rail and canal hub, and even on the river in the heart of downtown. Toledo's second bridge can be seen in the background. The Fassett Street Bridge was constructed in 1896 and located upriver from the Cherry Street Bridge. Even before it opened, its flimsy appearance disturbed many and prompted the city to make a public demonstration of its soundness. The city's heaviest vehicle, a horse-drawn steam driven water pumper (steamer), was pulled across the bridge at full speed. When a 1957 storm tore a large freighter loose from its moorings, it crashed into the bridge collapsing a portion of the structure. Later it was abandoned and removed.

Beginning in the late 1870s, Toledo became a major coal shipping port with at least four different railroads bringing soft coal from the fields of southeastern Ohio and West Virginia to the Maumee River loading docks. The Toledo & Ohio Central Railroad also had extensive iron ore unloading facilities directly opposite downtown where International Park is today.

One of The Iron ore Docks, Toledo, Ohio. 7/12 '08

18

B & O DOCKS

Bird's Eye View Toledo Shipyards, Toledo, Ohio.   11914

SHIPYARDS

With Toledo's prime location on Lake Erie, it is not surprising that shipbuilding became an important industry in the city. In 1881 the Bailey Shipyard, located at Ash and Summit streets, built the David Dows, the largest sailing vessel ever produced on the Great Lakes. In 1888 Captain John Craig and his son George established the Craig Shipbuilding Company, with yards on Front and Craig streets in East Toledo. Their first ship was launched in 1890. The plant expanded regularly until it was taken over by the Toledo Shipbuilding Company in 1905.

105. SCENE ON MAUMEE BAY, TOLEDO, OHIO

47114

MAUMEE BAY

The Baltimore & Ohio and the Hocking Valley railroads also had large coal and iron ore handling facilities on the Maumee. For several years in the late teens and early 1920s, Toledo shipped more coal than any other port in the United States—approximately eight million tons annually. By 1929 the Hocking Valley Railroad developed a new six million dollar state-of-the-art coal and iron ore facility at Presque Isle on Maumee Bay. Toledo then had one of the best combinations of rail and lake shipping terminals on the Great Lakes.

NO.64. VIEW OF THE WAYS AFTER LAUNCHING STR. FRED G HARTWELL. AT THE
TOLEDO SHIPBUILDING CO YARDS. TOLEDO. O. APRIL 4. 08.

PHOTO BY LA RUSH.

SHIP LAUNCHING

Toledo Shipbuilding eventually built and serviced many of the largest commercial vessels on the Great Lakes. Here they have just launched the Fred G. Hartwell in 1908.

12641   STR. "GREYHOUND" PASSING THROUGH CHERRY STREET BRIDGE, TOLEDO, OHIO.

STEAMER GREYHOUND

In addition to moving grain, coal, iron ore, and all manner of commercial goods, Toledoans used the waterways to move themselves. Water transportation was still one of the easiest ways to get from one place to another. A thriving business in commercial passenger steamboats developed. Luxury steamers left several times a day from the downtown Toledo riverfront for quick trips to Sandusky, Cedar Point, the Bass Islands, Monroe, Detroit, and points north.* The best-known passenger steamer serving Toledo was the Greyhound. Launched in 1902, she was huge—387 feet long, with a capacity of 3,366 persons—and over the thirty years she was in service, carried close to fourteen million passengers. Seen here passing through the Cherry Street Bridge, the Greyhound usually made two cruises daily—an all-day trip to Detroit or Cedar Point, followed by a moonlight cruise to Maumee Bay. The Greyhound would leave the Madison Avenue dock at 8:00 p.m., sail slowly past the bridges into the Bay, and slowly return about 11:00 p.m., all while an orchestra played for dancing. The popularity of the steamers began to decline as automobiles became more numerous. Most of the boats began to shut down after the First World War. Serving Toledo from 1917 to 1930, the Greyhound was the only remaining cruise ship of its kind. The Depression of 1929 brought the era of the passenger steamer on the Great Lakes to an end.

* The typical fare from Toledo to Detroit was $1.00.

STEAMER CITY OF TOLEDO

The proudest of the passenger steamers for local citizens was the City of Toledo, built by the Craig Shipbuilding Company. Launched in 1891, the steamer was 212 feet long, had three decks with six staterooms on each side and a cabin made of finished oak. It cost $140,000. During her first years, the City of Toledo made runs to Put-in-Bay and Middle Bass Island. In 1893 she went to Chicago and spent the summer on Lake Michigan, carrying passengers from downtown Chicago to Jackson Park for the great World's Columbian Exposition. She returned to the Toledo/Put-in-Bay route until sold by her owner, A.W. Colton, to the White Star Line of Detroit in 1896.

27. N. Y. C. TERMINAL, TOLEDO, OHIO.

THE MIDDLEGROUNDS

From the start, the focus of Toledo's riverfront commerce surrounded the foot of Monroe Street, where Swan Creek flows into the Maumee River. Ships could dock easily there and meet canal boats from Indiana and southern Ohio which floated down Swan Creek to the site. When the railroads began to transport more goods, they came there too. In the 1850s the Lake Shore and Michigan Southern Railroad (which later merged with the New York Central) filled and developed a large, swampy area along the river on the south side of Swan Creek. They built docks, elevators, warehouses, and Toledo's first significant rail station. These combined with a hotel—the Island House*—concentrated rail shipping and services at the very place served by lake and canal shippers. The filled area came to be known as "The Middlegrounds" (shown here) and, until the arrival of industry, the area was the hub of the city's economic livelihood.

* The Island House was Toledo's first major building.

MIAMI AND ERIE CANAL

The Erie Canal, which opened in 1825, carried people and goods from the Hudson River at Albany to the east end of Lake Erie at Buffalo. Continuing west across Lake Erie, the Maumee River provided the next link to the interior of the Midwest. The Wabash & Erie Canal to Indiana (1843) and the Miami & Erie Canal to Cincinnati (1845) were completed. These canals allowed further passage to the Ohio River, the Mississippi River, and the Gulf of Mexico. Toledo was on the main route of the vast interior waterway transportation system, connecting all parts of the country. The Ohio canals remained operational to and from Toledo until 1913 when one of the most devastating floods in Ohio's history damaged them beyond repair.

Lake Shore Limited in Train Yard, Union Depot, Toledo, Ohio.

25404

TRAIN YARD

Enterprising Toledo businessmen embraced the idea of bringing a railroad to Toledo. In 1836 local entrepreneurs successfully started the first railroad in the United States west of the Allegheny Mountains. The Erie & Kalamazoo Railroad* was primitive and unprofitable, eventually went bankrupt, and was sold in 1847. It did demonstrate that Toledo was serious about becoming a transportation and shipping center. The subsequent development of the Middlegrounds by the Lake Shore and Michigan Southern Railroad confirmed that.

* The Erie & Kalamazoo Railroad was never built as far as Kalamazoo, Michigan but did reach 33 miles from Toledo to Adrian, Michigan.

70730 UNION STATION, TOLEDO, OHIO   COPR. DETROIT PUBLISHING CO.

UNION STATION

The Middlegrounds site was low-lying and subject to flooding by the Maumee River. In 1883 the highest flood of record took place. It swept away the first Cherry Street Bridge and flooded the Middlegrounds, severely damaging the train station and destroying the contents of the warehouses and elevators. The Island House Hotel was flooded. After being trapped overnight, the guests had to be rescued by boat from the second floor windows. The New York Central Railroad decided to move its station to higher ground south of the Middlegrounds. The new Union Station opened in 1886 and remained in service until 1950.

TERMINAL·EXPOSITION·BLDG
TOLEDO, OHIO
MORE·GROUND·FLOOR·SPACE·THAN
MADISON·SQUARE·GARDEN

TERMINAL STATION

AUDITORIUM

In order to encourage business and solidify Toledo's status as a true rail hub, local interests formed The Toledo Railway and Terminal Company to build a loop connecting with every railroad entering the city. The company built its own station on Cherry Street. The Terminal Station operated as planned but it failed to become a common hub for many of the railroads. The building was converted into an exposition hall. As the postcard shows, it offered more floor space than Madison Square Garden in New York. The interior featured an auditorium claiming a seating capacity of 5,000.

DELIVERY WAGON

As the twentieth century dawned there were only 8,000 automobiles in the entire country. Toledo businesses relied on horsepower to move goods and supplies. This postcard depicts one of the delivery wagons of the B.R. Baker Company, 435-441 Summit Street.

DOCTOR SASS

With so many horses, livery stables were common—even in downtown Toledo—and blacksmithing was still an important service. Veterinarians such as Herman F. Sass, shown here in front of his animal hospital at 232-234 Vine Street, were also needed. This postcard portrays the most common forms of transportation in Toledo in 1908, including an early automobile.

GENDRON

WIRE WHEELS

This photo postcard pictures children demonstrating some of Gendron's creations in front of a residence at the corner of Orchard and Hawley streets. Gendron products became well-known and were sold all over the country. Toledo became the country's leader in the manufacture of bicycles. In the 1890s nearly two dozen factories in the city made bicycles, wheels, and other parts, earning the city the nickname of "The Coventry of America" for its parallel with the English town of that name known throughout Europe for similar products.

Before the automobile, Toledo's preoccupation with transportation had made it one of the country's leading bicycle manufacturers. Peter Gendron was one of the leaders in developing the industry and the inventor of the first practical wire-spoked wheel. From the 1890s to the 1930s, he built and sold various bicycles, tricycles, wheeled invalid chairs, baby carriages, coaster wagons, doll buggies, and toy wheelbarrows from a large four-story factory at the corner of Superior and Orange streets.

WAGON MAKER

Toledo was also in the forefront of building animal-drawn vehicles. The city's first truly large manufacturing plant was the Milburn Wagon Works, one of the largest wagon-makers in the country. In 1873 a group of civic-minded Toledo businessmen raised $300,000 to lure brothers, George and John Milburn, and their wagon-making business from Indiana. Thirty-two acres were purchased for them on Monroe Street west of Detroit Avenue.

A MILBURN WAGON

Milburn built a large factory on the site and began turning out all types of wagons and carriages in 1875. Here is an example of a fire wagon with the factory in the background. The Milburn Works was once the largest producer of farm wagons in the country. During World War I, the company had a government contract to produce ambulances—one of the last large commissions before the automobile rendered most of their products obsolete.

ELECTRIC CAR

In an attempt to update its products, Milburn tried its hand first at producing electric trucks and then passenger cars like the 1917 Milburn Electric model shown here. As demand for wagons decreased after World War I, the main plant gradually began to shut down. After a devastating fire in 1919, Milburn Wagon Works eventually closed.

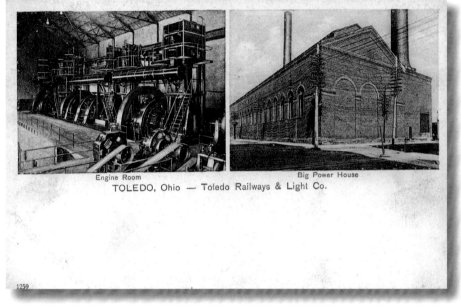

Engine Room   Big Power House

TOLEDO, Ohio — Toledo Railways & Light Co.

POWER HOUSE

The first practical use of electricity in Toledo was in the 1890s when the new power source was utilized to run trolley cars. After a period of competition and consolidation, a number of trolley companies merged into the Community Traction Company in 1895-96. The new company built its first big coal-fired generating plant on the riverfront at the foot of Madison Avenue. When it opened, the power house was one of the largest in the country. Its original purpose was to supply electricity to run the company's 250 trolleys, but it also generated power for many thousands of lights on both sides of the river. The company was the city's main source of electricity until the larger Acme Power Company plant was completed on the East Side in 1918. By 1930 the original plant stopped generating electricity and was converted to produce steam heat for downtown buildings. The facility closed in 1985.

THE LONG BELT

In 1901 the Toledo Railways and Light Company, also known as T.R.&L., not only acquired all of the trolley lines, but also began a process (over the next few years) of buying many of the artificial gas, electric, and heating utility companies. The company also acquired many of the electrical street railways in the areas around Toledo. T.R.&L. operated the trolleys until 1921 when a newly re-formed Community Traction Company assumed that part of the business. T.R.&L. then changed its name to Toledo Edison and concentrated on providing electricity and related utilities. The Long Belt route was, as the name implies, the longest of the trolley loops.* This route served so many riders that it remained on the schedule until trolley service was discontinued at the end of 1949. Fares were generally five cents but controversy over rates was constant and led to strikes, violence, and political debate.

* The Long Belt route began at Summit Street and ran out Monroe Street, past the Milburn Wagon Works to serve the Auburndale neighborhood, on to Auburn Avenue, north to Central Avenue at Woodlawn Cemetery, then east passing the Pope-Toledo plant (later Willys-Overland), on to Collingwood Boulevard (Avenue), then south to Ashland Avenue angling to Adams Street, and into downtown to Summit Street to complete the loop.

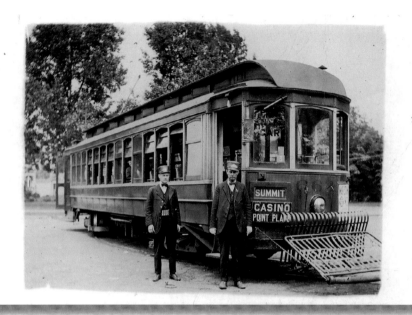

CASINO RIDE

The Toledo Railways and Light Company purchased and operated several of the major entertainment attractions in the Toledo area such as the Toledo Beach Company and the Lake Erie Park and Casino, also known as the Toledo Casino or the Casino. T.R.&L. enjoyed a monopoly on the transportation to these destinations as they were accessible only by their trolley lines. In the summertime, cars such as this one on the Point Place run would leave every few minutes from downtown, taking customers out Summit Street to the Casino on Maumee Bay. Customers would pay 15 cents for the ride, which included "free" admission to the Casino.*

* For more information about the Casino, see Chapter 8.

ACCIDENT

Of course, with so many trolleys, there were bound to be accidents. In this 1908 incident, the swing bridge over Swan Creek at Erie Street failed to close as the Erie-Western trolley approached. The driver managed to avert the disaster that would have befallen the occupants if the car had gone into the water. The message written on the back of this postcard says: "How would you like to have been in this car. No one was hurt as it balanced on the edge and did not go over. Father and Loren were both in it. Your friend, Alva."

INTERURBAN

For a decade or more immediately before and after the dawn of the twentieth century, trolleys were the gold standard of transportation in the Toledo area. Electric railway lines then sprang up and began radiating out to nearby cities. Toledo became one of the busiest electric interurban hubs in the Midwest, with over a dozen lines running north to Detroit; east to Cleveland via Fremont, Sandusky, Norwalk, and Lorain; south to Findlay, Lima, and Dayton; and west to Bryan and to northern Indiana. The local stations occupied several buildings over the years in downtown on Superior Street.

BOODY HOUSE

Business leaders recognized the importance of having a grand hotel to impress the many travelers and businessmen coming to town. When it was constructed at the southwest corner of Madison Avenue and St. Clair Street, the Boody House became the dominant feature of the downtown skyline. Built in a grandiose French Second Empire style in 1872, it had all the amenities available in the 1870s—a passenger elevator, a sink with hot and cold running water in every one of its 150 rooms, and a bathroom with a water closet on every floor. It was the premier venue for social events and hosted almost every important traveler of the nineteenth century, including every president from Ulysses S. Grant to William Howard Taft.

PRODUCE EXCHANGE

Directly across Madison Avenue from the Boody House was the Produce Exchange Building. It was built in 1878 to house the local grain merchants' futures market.

FEDERAL BUILDING

Completed in 1888, the Federal Office Building housed Toledo's central post office until about 1911. The Federal Building remained a prominent downtown landmark and remained in use until 1962. It was located on the current site of Levis Square.

Bird's eye view~Toledo, O.

TOLEDO 1890

Three buildings were the anchors of a city about to embark on a new phase of growth and development. They were built at the same intersection of Madison Avenue and St. Clair Street—the Boody House, the Produce Exchange, and the Federal Building. This chapter has attempted to convey the spirit and activity in Toledo by the early 1890s. The city was on the eve of its transition to a stage of development based on the impending arrival of new industry and manufacturing. This postcard shows downtown Toledo from the east side of the Maumee River. The Cherry Street Bridge is the large bridge in the center.

CHAPTER THREE
THE ARRIVAL OF INDUSTRY

For much of the nineteenth century, Toledo's industry developed along lines similar to those experienced by most of the new cities in the American interior. But that was about to change.

One of Toledo's successes in this pre-industrial era was the Woolson Spice Company. It was founded in 1882 by grocer and coffee merchant Alvin M. Woolson. His company produced exotic spices and teas along with their most noted product—coffee. In addition to his economic contributions to Toledo's development, Woolson was a prominent civic leader who participated in many of the city's important social and philanthropic endeavors. He was one of the earliest sponsors of the Toledo Newsboys' Association and an early member and benefactor of the Toledo Museum of Art.[1] Perhaps his most significant accomplishment though was his role in gathering a group of Toledo businessmen called the "Citizens' Committee," a forerunner of the Chamber of Commerce. These men encouraged industries to move to Toledo. The formation of the Citizens' Committee proved to be one of the pivotal strategies in the city's development.

Toledo business leaders realized that attracting big industry would require easy access to raw materials and fuel. While Toledo itself did not possess abundant supplies of either, its centralized location and highly-developed transportation and shipping facilities gave it the ability to bring in resources economically. In those pre-electricity times, industrial equipment was driven largely by steam, which was produced predominantly by burning coal. So Toledo businessmen moved swiftly to make Toledo a successful coal-shipping center. They built or financed four different railroads to the coal fields of southeastern Ohio and western Pennsylvania.

In 1884 a large natural gas reservoir under high pressure was discovered in Findlay, about fifty miles south of Toledo. At first the force and seemingly endless supply of gas energized the residents of northwestern Ohio. They thought for at least a short time that the new fuel source would immediately attract industry from far and wide, including the iron and steel manufacturers from Cleveland and Pittsburgh. The City of Findlay even burned natural gas to illuminate their entire town day and night, and businesspeople in Toledo began building pipelines to the city. For a time, hyperbole was rampant—Toledo was no longer a "future great," but was already a "present great" due to natural gas.

In 1887 the Citizens' Committee placed advertisements in newspapers around the country seeking to attract new industries. They emphasized Toledo's location in a network of railroads and steamship lines as well as its ability to provide coal, oil, and natural gas less expensively than in the East. For the benefit of glassmakers, they mentioned the nearby quantities of sandstone with high silica content for making high-quality glass. At the time Edward Drummond Libbey, who had recently inherited the New England Glass Company from his father, was experiencing a combination of labor difficulties, high marketing and shipping costs, and skyrocketing fuel and material costs in the East. The Toledo advertisements attracted Libbey's attention. After negotiating for incentives[2], he signed a contract on February 6, 1888, to move his glassmaking operations to Toledo. The glass industry would become the local promoters' greatest success.

The most significant outcome was that Libbey's success and the advantages of the northwestern Ohio location soon began to draw other glassmakers. The most important was Edward Ford. His father, Captain John Ford, had founded the Pittsburgh Plate Glass Company. Mr. Ford came to Wood County just south of Toledo in 1898 to build a state-of-the-art factory to make cast-polished plate glass for windows. By 1900 this plant was the largest plate glassmaker in the country.

---

1. The Toledo Museum of Art was founded on April 18, 1901.

2. Libbey received $4,000 to purchase four acres for his plant as well as 50 lots for workers' homes.

Another piece in the development of the glass industry came with a veritable revolution in bottle making—the result of the engineering genius of Libbey employee and manager, Michael J. Owens. Owens invented the first mechanical bottle making machine.[3] In 1903 Libbey formed the Owens Bottle Machine Company to make and lease these machines rather than selling them outright. This step allowed the Toledo directors to control glass container production all over the world. By the early 1920s, in fact, 94 out of every 100 bottles made worldwide were produced on Owens machines. In 1929 Owens Bottle Company merged with Illinois Glass to form Owens-Illinois, the largest bottle making firm in the world. Michael Owens' brilliant skills were also used to automate and improve the production of plate glass to allow the making of continuous glass sheets, bettering a machine invented by Irving M. Colburn. The savings in time and preparation revolutionized the flat glass segment of the industry.

In 1930 the great glassmaking triumvirate merged sheet glass-making operations into Libbey-Owens-Ford and that company has been in continuous operation since. Toledo's success in attracting the glass industry was its biggest overall contribution to the development of the city's industrial era.

The invention of the automobile had a revolutionary impact on the transportation industry and Toledo's development. Easterner Albert A. Pope, the country's largest bicycle maker at the end of the nineteenth century, started producing a gasoline-powered automobile in 1903 in a former bicycle plant on Central Avenue in Toledo. For several years the Pope-Toledo automobile, a more expensive luxury model, was well-known all over the country and even abroad. Pope's company, which employed 1,200 to 1,500 workers, went into receivership in 1907. In 1909 Pope sold the Toledo plant to John North Willys, an automobile salesman from Elmira, New York. Willys helped refinance and save the troubled Overland Company in Indianapolis a few years earlier in order to protect his sales orders. The Toledo plant was large enough to handle Willys-Overland's expansion needs, and in a few years—much to the economic advantage of Toledo—it was producing huge numbers of automobiles. By 1923 the Toledo plant was the largest automobile factory in the world. At its peak Willys-Overland employed more than 20,000 workers and produced 22,000 vehicles per month. In 1927 over 300,000 cars were produced at the Central Avenue plant.

The economic impact on the city went far beyond Willys-Overland being Toledo's largest employer for much of the twentieth century. The city's proximity to Detroit made it an ideal location for producing auto parts and accessories to supply both the Toledo and Detroit plants. Many parts makers followed Willys to the area—including Kinsey Manufacturing (auto sheet metal components), Warner Manufacturing Company (gears and transmissions), Electric Auto-Lite (starters, generators, and other electrical equipment), Champion Spark Plug (which eventually became the world's largest manufacturer of spark plugs), Spicer Manufacturing (transmissions), and AP Parts (shock absorbers, exhaust pipes, and so forth), to name a few of the largest companies. Even the glass industry participated as Libbey-Owens-Ford became a leader in the production of window glass for automobiles.

Some estimates suggest that automobile-related manufacturing accounted for more than 40 percent of the total payroll of the Toledo workforce during a large part of the 1920s. These manufacturers required workers, bringing many job seekers to Toledo. Many of these were immigrants and their families who established several distinct ethnic neighborhoods within the city. Census figures identify more than 40 ethnic groups in Toledo by the first few decades of the twentieth century. During that time nearly two-thirds of Toledo's residents were either foreign-born or had at least one parent who was. These groups all worked hard to live the "American Dream" and did their best to assimilate and participate in the new American way of life. But they also retained many of their own social and cultural practices that enriched the city's character.

3. For more information about Michael J. Owens, see Chapter 4.

32

BUCKEYE BEER

Toledo-based Buckeye Brewery began operations in 1838, just one year after the city was incorporated. It operated for 134 years until it was purchased by the Miller Brewing Company in 1972.* Buckeye claimed to be the oldest industry in Toledo and the second oldest brewery in America.+ From humble beginnings, the company grew into a major producer of beer by the 1870s. Buckeye anticipated future trends by building its own bottling plant at Michigan and Bush streets in 1895, improving upon the older practice of carrying beer home from the brewery in a growler.# Buckeye survived the years of Prohibition by brewing a "near beer," bottling soft drinks, and offering its facilities to others for cold storage. Buckeye was the only Toledo brewery to survive World War II. This 1910 advertising postcard for Buckeye's famous

Green Seal Beer explains on the back that drinking two pint bottles of this beer would not make you an alcoholic. Rather, as "prominent chemists" attest, it would furnish nourishment the equivalent of twelve ounces of potatoes, eight ounces of meat, five ounces of bread, or one pint of milk.

* Miller Lite, one of the most popular beers in America, was originally Buckeye's copyrighted formula.
\+ The Toledo Blade began publishing in 1837 and is Toledo's oldest continuously operating business.
\# A growler is a pitcher, pail, or other container brought by a customer for beer.

BIERZENTANKEN

One of Buckeye's main competitors was John Huebner. In 1896 he acquired the City Brewing and Malting Company, originally founded by Toledo's great pioneer businessman Peter Lenk. He changed the name to the Huebner Brewing Company. In 1905 it merged with other local breweries to form a conglomerate under the name of Huebner-Toledo Breweries Company. Huebner then took over the former Finlay Brewery, shown here, on North Summit Street near downtown. He soon became the largest brewer in town. The competition with Buckeye and other local breweries was fierce for many years.

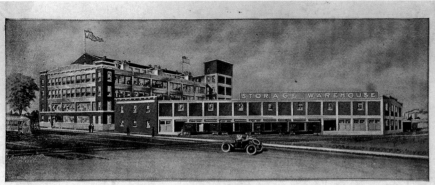

THIS is our new home—re-inforced concrete construction and absolutely fireproof—completed November, 1911. We proudly point to it as the greatest institution of its kind in the world. It puts into expression the very latest ideas, methods and processes for roasting and blending fine coffee, for blending choice tea, for the manufacture of pure spices. We welcome our customers.

THE WOOLSON SPICE COMPANY TOLEDO OHIO

WOOLSON SPICE

For many years the Woolson Spice Company factory and offices were located in a large building on the southeastern corner of Jackson and Huron streets, allowing the pleasing aroma of roasting coffee to spread all over downtown. By 1911 the business had outgrown the downtown location and a large modern factory complex was opened at 2700 North Summit Street near the river. For several decades two companies—the Arbuckle Company of Pittsburgh and Woolson Spice Company of Toledo—supplied almost all of the coffee consumed in the United States.

LION COFFEE

Woolson's signature brand was "Lion Coffee." It was known all over the country and millions of pounds were sold. Alvin Woolson was the first to package the coffee in one-pound bags—a practice all of the other producers immediately copied. Over the years the company also sold packaged teas and developed the market for a variety of spices from around the world.

MIDSUMMER GREETING

Woolson was one of the first to offer premiums as incentives to customers. Picture cards, such as this one, were included in every pound package of coffee. Woolson vice president N.L. Schmid described the program for The Toledo Blade in 1951: "On each package was a lion's head and they were good for premiums of all sorts. Circulars listing premiums were placed in the packages and I remember when the incoming mail was so heavy that we had to send our own truck to the post office to pick it up. We employed as high as 35 or 40 girls whose only duties were to open letters and packages containing the lion heads. Instead of counting the coupons we weighed them to determine the number....Among the premiums were suitcases, lamps, lace curtains, jackknives, and bicycles. Some individuals who made it their business to go through the country buying the lion heads would deliver as many as 8,000 or 10,000 and in redeeming them would take our entire supply of suitcases."

LIBBEY GLASS

Toledo provided Edward Drummond Libbey a four-acre site for his factory on Buckeye Street and 50 building lots for workers' homes. By summer 1888 the plant was nearly completed. Libbey and his workforce arrived by train at Toledo's new Union Station to a rousing reception and a parade to the factory. A banquet was held and Toledo welcomed what would become one of the city's greatest acquisitions.

Courtesy of the Libbey Glass Company, American, Punch Bowl and Stand and 23 Cups, 1903-4, glass, Toledo Museum of Art, Gift of Owens-Illinois Company, 1946.27

DAZZLING

EXPANDED PLANT

Despite the excitement and fanfare, the Libbey plant struggled for several years. Libbey survived only because a strike at Corning Glass Works in Corning, New York, enabled him to make lightbulbs for General Electric. In a desperate gamble, he set up a working model of a glass factory as an exhibit at the 1893 Chicago World's Fair. The fortunes of the company were turned around. The marketing success of the World's Fair was a lesson not lost on Libbey and other Toledo businessmen, many of whom exhibited Toledo products at future fairs and expositions. Here is the famous punch bowl created by Libbey's artisan, J. Rufus Denman, for display at the St. Louis World's Fair in 1904. The bowl is now on display at the Toledo Museum of Art.

By the time this 1910 postcard was printed, the Toledo plant had become the largest cut glass factory in the world. In addition, Libbey's success attracted other glassmakers to Toledo. As these industries came and new innovations in technology were developed, Libbey cooperated with them to create and expand many of the most important segments in the manufacture of glass. By the late 1920s, these cooperative efforts made Toledo "The Glass Capital of the World."

Rossford Plant of Libbey-Owens-Ford Glass Company, Toledo, Ohio

LIBBEY-OWENS-FORD

Edward Ford of the Pittsburgh Plate Glass family was impressed by the advantages of glassmaking in the Toledo area. In 1898 he purchased 160 acres on the east side of the Maumee River, just south of the Toledo limits. There he built a large state-of-the-art plate glass manufacturing plant which soon became the largest and most advanced in the country. As one of the old school patrician capitalists, he adhered to the practice of creating a whole community around the plant. Homes and services were created in the new community of Rossford for the benefit of his workers and their families. After 1910 Michael J. Owens turned his talents to the plate glass portion of the business as well. Owens and other engineers perfected a method previously developed by Irving M. Colburn to produce sheets of glass in a continuous flow. He formed the Libbey-Owens Sheet Glass Company to produce plate glass in 1916. In 1930 this company merged with Edward Ford's Rossford plant to form Libbey-Owens-Ford, a true giant in the plate glass industry.

Toledo Furnace Company. Toledo, Ohio.

TOLEDO FURNACE

Toledo also attracted a number of substantial iron and steel smelting and casting operations in the 1890s. These included the Smead Furnace & Foundry Company at Bancroft and Smead streets, the National Malleable Castings Plant on Front Street, and the large foundry of the Toledo Furnace Company, shown here, at 2401 Front Street.

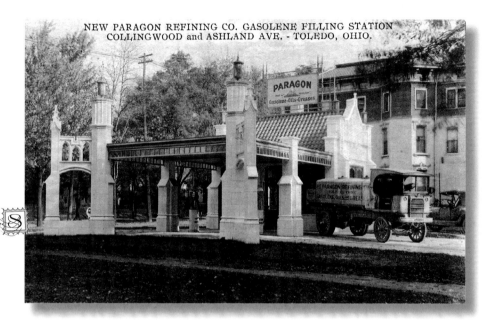

GAS STATION GEM

John D. Rockefeller's Standard Oil Company controlled the vast majority of Ohio's oil business. It built its own refinery on Otter Creek Road in East Toledo. Several smaller companies also developed local refining operations. In 1888 the Paragon Refining Company built the first one in Ironville at Front Street near Millard Avenue. Paragon sold its gasoline and related oil products around the Toledo area, including at this architectural gem of an early gas station.

NATIONAL SUPPLY COMPANY

In 1890 both the Craig and Sun Oil Companies also opened refineries in Toledo. While Toledo did not become the principal oil-refining center of the Midwest, it did develop a respectable share of the business. Toledo also became an important center for providing oil field and drilling supplies. Among the supply companies were the Acme Sucker Rod Company, owned by future Toledo Mayor Samuel "Golden Rule" Jones, and The National Supply Company, shown here in downtown Toledo. Located at Washington and St. Clair streets, it was one of the largest oil industry supply companies in the United States. The taller building presently houses the offices of the Toledo Mud Hens and the Toledo Walleye.

POPE-TOLEDO

Toledo's first attempt at manufacturing automobiles was made by Albert A. Pope, owner of the American Bicycle Company, the largest maker of bicycles in the country. Pope's holdings included a plant on Central Avenue west of Detroit Avenue which had previously manufactured sewing machines, marine motors, bicycles, and even an early attempt at a steam-powered carriage called the "Toledo." In 1902 Pope converted the factory for making an expensive luxury gasoline-powered automobile he called the "Pope-Toledo." Despite its high cost, the Pope-Toledo was fairly successful for five years. It was known far and wide and even had sales in Europe. It competed in a number of races and generally fared well. This is one of the company's last models—the Type XII from 1907.

707—WILLYS OVERLAND AUTOMOBILE PLANT, TOLEDO, OHIO.

WILLYS-OVERLAND

The person most responsible for the development of the automobile industry in Toledo was John North Willys (1873-1935). When he was 25 years old he ran a bicycle business that grossed a half a million dollars a year. In 1906 and 1907, he sold over 500 automobiles for the Overland Company of Indiana. When that company floundered, he bailed it out by raising enough money to keep it going. He gradually gained control, reorganized the company, and made it profitable. When the closed Pope plant in Toledo became available in 1909, Willys bought it. He moved the Overland Company into it in 1911 and rapidly expanded its operations. Willys renamed the enterprise the Willys-Overland Motor Company in 1912. Remarkably, by 1915, Willys-Overland was producing more automobiles than anyone in America with the exception of Henry Ford.

Principal Factories and Administration Building of The Willys-Overland Company, Toledo, Ohio, Builders of Overland and Willys-Knight Motor Cars.

Largest single automobile factory in the world.

4,486,680 square feet of factory floor space—equal to 103 acres, or 36 average city blocks, 250 x 500 feet.

17,000 factory employees; eight-hour day.

12⅓ miles of railroad tracks in the factory yards.

Largest drop-forging plant in the industry—85 steam hammers.

125,000 tons of steel used in a year.

Largest users of aluminum in the world—more than 15,000,000 pounds used in a year.

WILLYS' STATISTICS

By 1916 one out of every five wage earners in Toledo worked at the Willys-Over-land plant. By 1918, the plant had become the largest single automobile factory in the world. It had grown to 4.5 million square feet (103 acres) under roof.

FINAL ASSEMBLY

These Willys-Overland workers are shown in the final assembly room with one of their products on September 16, 1912.

MODEL 59-T

HEADQUARTERS

By 1915 Willys built an office headquarters and administration building that was, as the postcard boasts, the largest single-tenant office building in Ohio. Other postcards reveal it had seven stories, nearly 160,000 square feet of floor space, four fast passenger elevators, a large freight elevator, a telegraph office, an automatic mail conveyor carrying 22,000 pieces of mail per day, and a private telephone exchange connecting over 500 departments and handling more than 10,000 calls per day. The building also featured a large cafeteria and an 800-seat auditorium.

OVERLAND DELIVERY VAN

Because of competition with other makers, Overland developed many types and models of vehicles. One of their delivery trucks from about 1915 is shown here.

Train over a mile long loaded with Overlands. It requires over 30 such trainloads daily to ship the plant's output.
A vista of chassis. The enlarged plant is turning out 1,000 daily.

SHIPPING 1,000 CARS A DAY AT WILLYS-OVERLAND PLANT, TOLEDO, OHIO.

1,000 DAILY

Throughout the 1920s the plant continued to expand. As this postcard shows, production reached a level of one thousand cars per day.

NEW SUPERIOR **WHIPPET SIX**
COACH $**695**
f.o.b. Toledo

Your Name and Address Here

WHIPPET SIX

By 1925 the Willys-Overland payroll of $27-million represented 41 percent of the entire payroll of the City of Toledo. In 1927 Willys-Overland introduced its Whippet Six model which created a sensation in the industry because it sold for under $700. In 1928, the plant had its biggest year, employing up to 23,000 workers and manufacturing 314,437 cars. Production became so aggressive that the company found itself outstripping demand for its units. By April, 1929, six months before the stock market crashed, Willys-Overland was forced to begin laying off workers. As the summer wore on, as many as 10,000 employees were already living on their savings. The more than 30 local parts supply plants then had to follow suit. Toledo suffered a serious unemployment problem several months before the onset of the Great Depression. That unemployment ensured that when the financial crisis of October struck, the impact on Toledo would be even greater than in many other places around the country. Through all the ups and downs, however, there is no doubt that the contribution of John North Willys to the development and growth of Toledo's economy was enormous. The Willys-Overland plant was the longest operating automobile factory in the history of the country. In addition, it was Toledo's largest employer for nearly a century and attracted satellite manufacturers of auto parts and supplies.

AUTO-LITE

In 1911 Electric Auto-Lite was started by Clement O. Miniger. Auto-Lite produced starters and generators for Willys-Overland vehicles. In 1914 Willys bought controlling interest of the fledgling Electric Auto-Lite Corporation. Miniger remained president and later bought out Willys. These companies and several dozen others helped turn Toledo into a specialized auto parts center, eventually accounting for over a third of all the jobs and industrial output of the city.

CHAMPION

In 1910 brothers Robert A. and Frank D. Stranahan came to Toledo and established the Champion Spark Plug Company. The business grew to become the largest spark plug manufacturer in the world. Here a Champion sponsored automobile visits Independence Hall in Philadelphia as part of a series of postcards promoting the Champion name at various landmarks around the country.

GOOD SHEPHERD

As a new and rapidly expanding city, Toledo attracted large numbers of foreign-born residents during all phases of its development. In the middle of the nineteenth century, the city's first wave of immigrants included Irish victims of the terrible potato famines of the 1840s. Many found work building the Wabash and Erie Canal. These immigrant groups tended to congregate in distinct neighborhoods and develop their own social networks, often centering on their churches. St. Patrick's at the southern edge of downtown and Good Shepherd on the east side of the river served the Irish community.

ST. PATRICK'S

LADIES AID

Until 1920 German settlers were the most numerous immigrant group in Toledo. The Germans were active from the start in promoting the development of the city. Brewer and winemaker Peter Lenk platted a whole new city addition in the south end, while Rudolph Bartley established the city's largest wholesale grocery operation. Many Germans were prominent community leaders, including four who became mayor.* The Ladies Aid of the First Reformed (German) Church, Canton Avenue and Scott Street, gather here for a 1909 outing at Point Place. The congregation was organized in 1853 and moved into a late Victorian Gothic style church designed by the important Toledo architect Edward O. Fallis in 1882. Though vacant, the building still stands.

* The four German-born mayors and the years elected were William Kraus (1869), Guido Marx (1875), Jacob Romeis (1879), and George Scheets (1885).

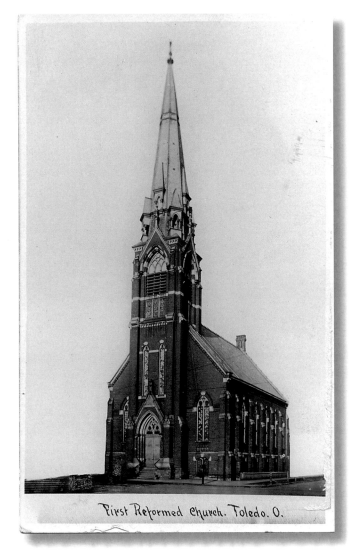

FIRST REFORMED

POLE TO POLE

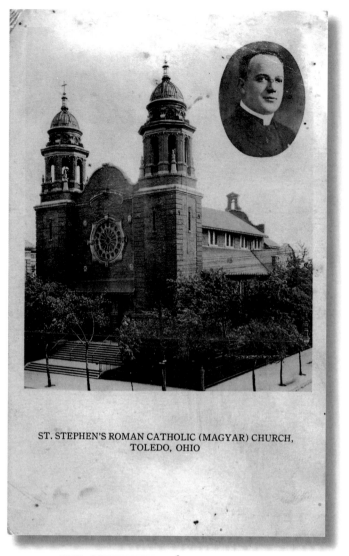

ST. STEPHEN'S ROMAN CATHOLIC (MAGYAR) CHURCH,
TOLEDO, OHIO

ST. STEPHEN'S CHURCH

After 1880 another wave of immigration began, this time consisting largely of people from eastern and southern Europe who were fleeing unrest, violence, and poverty in their native lands. Poles began arriving in Toledo in large numbers beginning around 1890. They settled and established two separate neighborhoods. One was south along Nebraska Avenue beyond Peter Lenk's original German addition and was known as Kuschwantz. The other in the north end of town along Lagrange Street was called Lagrinka. Each section built its own major church around which charitable, social, and cultural affairs revolved—St. Anthony's on Nebraska Avenue and St. Hedwig's on Lagrange Street. Though separate, the two Polish neighborhoods retained close ties, and were even connected by a trolley line which some of the residents of the day humorously proclaimed must be the longest trolley line in the world since it stretched from "Pole to Pole."

In 1892 when the National Malleable Castings Company built its giant foundry on Front Street, the company brought about a hundred skilled Hungarian iron workers and their families from its operation in Cleveland. These families established a Hungarian neighborhood known as Birmingham. It has retained much of its Hungarian ethnic identity for over a century.

The Hungarians established St. Stephen's Catholic Parish and, around the time of the First World War, built St. Stephen's Roman Catholic (Magyar) Church. By 1920 the price of passage from Budapest had been lowered to the point that many Hungarians migrated here. Knowing of the Birmingham neighborhood, many came to Toledo, swelling the Hungarian population to more than 5,000.

CHAPTER FOUR

TOLEDO'S CONTRIBUTIONS TO A BETTER WORLD

At the turn of the twentieth century, the rapid growth of industry and technology and the need for new sources of power led to an explosion of creativity and new ideas. Nothing seemed impossible for inventors and entrepreneurs. Unprecedented concepts became reality. Toledoans and Toledo companies invented important new processes and products that made a lasting impact on American life and business. First, Toledo put its mark on the glass industry and then on the industries producing spray equipment, scales and automobiles. In addition, Toledoans were vital to the early development of aviation and radio communications.

As noted in the previous chapter, Michael J. Owens made the most significant contributions to technological innovation and had the greatest impact on Toledo's development as an industrial power. A mechanical genius with little formal education, Owens revolutionized the glass bottle industry. His bottle making machines dramatically increased production and allowed for the standardization of glass containers. He made similar contributions to flat glass production.

The remarkable DeVilbiss family originated the basic framework that gave birth to several industries. In 1888 Dr. Allen DeVilbiss invented the atomizer that facilitated application of medicine to patients' throats. Soon after, he formed the DeVilbiss Manufacturing Company to produce spray equipment. His son, Allen Jr., invented a springless automatic scale in 1897. He established the DeVilbiss Scale Company which eventually became the world famous Toledo Scale Company. The scales gave the world a new standard of accuracy in weights and measures. The doctor's other son, Thomas, contributed to the development of the spray gun and perfumizers. His spray gun revolutionized paint and lacquer application for furniture and automobile makers.

Toledo automobile companies and parts suppliers also contributed numerous innovations and improvements in automobile manu-

facturing technology. One example was John North Willys' incorporation of the sleeve valve[1] engine into the production of an affordable automobile. The sleeve valve was invented by Charles Y. Knight of Chicago in 1903. An engine incorporating sleeve valves was more efficient and quieter than the prevailing poppet valve[2] engine of the day. A disadvantage was the higher cost to manufacture, resulting in their use only for luxury automobiles. In 1913 Willys purchased the Edwards Motor Company of New York City. The acquisition included license to use the Knight sleeve valve. Realizing he had a valuable new asset, Willys immediately began to incorporate the technology into his products. Willys discovered ways to reduce the cost of manufacturing sleeve valve engines.

Toledo was in the forefront of some of the most important events related to the development of aviation. Around the turn of the twentieth century, A. Roy Knabenshue, a young Toledo inventor and engineer, began experimenting with powered balloons for manned flight. In 1904 he participated in the Aeronautic Competition at the Louisiana Purchase Exposition, commonly known as the St. Louis World's Fair. He competed in the free balloon races and met Captain Thomas Baldwin from California. Baldwin had built America's first dirigible, the *California Arrow*, and entered it in the competition. Knabenshue agreed to pilot the hydrogen-filled craft that was powered by a gasoline engine. He flew 11 miles in one hour and 31 minutes, winning the competition. His successful piloting of a powered dirigible was the first in the United States and one of the top attractions of the Fair. After the St. Louis World's Fair, Knabenshue signed on to pilot Baldwin's dirigible at fairs and exhibitions in

1. A sleeve valve is an intake or exhaust valve for an engine, consisting of one or more sleeves reciprocating within a cylinder, so that ports in the cylinder and in the sleeves are opposed at regular intervals to open the valve.

2. A poppet valve is a rising and falling valve consisting of a disk at the end of a vertically set stem, used in internal-combustion engines.

the West. He returned to Toledo in 1905 to design and build his own dirigible which he called *Toledo I*. The first flight of his powered air machine was a huge success. He flew from Toledo's Tri-State Fairgrounds on Dorr Street to downtown where he landed safely atop the Spitzer Building. Knabenshue built more dirigibles and formed a troupe that conducted flight exhibitions throughout the eastern United States for the next few years. In 1909 he joined other aviation pioneers, the Wright brothers, in planning and scheduling their public exhibitions. Roy Knabenshue was one of the true trailblazers in the emerging field of aviation.

Following his success at the Columbian Exposition in 1893, Edward Drummond Libbey also exhibited his glass products at the St. Louis World's Fair. Several other Toledo firms participated as well, including the new Toledo Scale Company.

A Western Union telegraph operator from Toledo named Frank Butler visited the St. Louis World's Fair. He came to learn about the technological wonders on display, particularly the electrical inventions of Thomas Edison. As a telegrapher, Butler was fascinated by the exhibit of the American de Forest Wireless Telegraph Company that demonstrated transmitting telegraph messages through the air. Butler immediately went to work for inventor Lee de Forest. Shortly after, de Forest and Butler were walking on the Fair grounds when de Forest noticed a dirigible piloted by Roy Knabenshue circling above them. When Butler told de Forest that Knabenshue was a Toledoan and an acquaintance of his, de Forest asked to be introduced to him. While in St. Louis, the three hit upon a way to combine their technical skills. The two Toledoans, Roy Knabenshue and Frank Butler, went up together in the dirigible along with de Forest's telegraph transmitter/receiver. Butler successfully received and transmitted the first ground-to-air and air-to-ground wireless messages in history.

Frank Butler continued to work with de Forest in his experiments in wireless telephony, the transmission of the human voice through the air without wires. It was Butler who coined the word "radio" to describe the process. By 1907 de Forest, with Butler's help, had developed the vacuum tube. It was a revolutionary device that could amplify a weak signal by the use of a tiny amount of electrical power. The vacuum tube made it possible to transmit signals over long distances for the first time. It became key to the development of communication by radio, and later by television and computer. The vacuum tube changed the world forever.

The first practical demonstration of wireless voice broadcasting took place on July 18, 1907, and also became the first ship-to-shore communication in history. Because of his familiarity with northwestern Ohio, Butler brought de Forest and the first radio broadcasting and receiving equipment to the annual Inter-Lake Yachting Association Regatta at Put-in-Bay on Lake Erie. De Forest boarded a yacht with a radio transmitter and witnessed the race. At the exact moment each yacht crossed the finish line, he reported the results to Butler on shore. The order of finish could then be relayed promptly to the newspapers. This historic event not only made de Forest the first sports broadcaster, it also made him the first disc jockey, as he played music from a record player between his race reports.

Butler brought the equipment back to Toledo for further demonstrations in the hope of attracting investors. On August 1, 1907, he arranged a successful wireless broadcast in downtown Toledo which became the first time that voice was transmitted from one building to another. While Lee de Forest is rightly credited for the key inventive work, Toledo and Toledo resident Frank Butler obviously played a significant role in one of the greatest technological achievements.

Lenk Wine Company, Toledo, Ohio.

LENK WINE COMPANY

In 1888 Dr. Allen DeVilbiss established the DeVilbiss Manufacturing Company. As the company grew, it moved into the abandoned Lenk Winery buildings on Detroit Avenue opposite Phillips Avenue. The company manufactured medical atomizers, perfumizers, and spray guns for painting applications. In the 1920s its product line expanded to include air compressors and exhaust booths for the automobile industry. In 1926 the name was changed to The DeVilbiss Company. The company had become a major manufacturing concern, selling its products all over the world.

Toledo Computing Scale Co., Toledo, Ohio.

TOLEDO SCALE COMPANY

Allen DeVilbiss, Jr. invented the first springless automatic computing scale for accurate weighing. His invention was an improvement on all existing scale designs. His Toledo Computing Scale Company was sold and became the Toledo Scale Company. The original plant, located at the intersection of Monroe and Albion streets west of the Milburn Wagon Works, was expanded several times. Finally it outgrew its location and was replaced by a huge modern complex on Telegraph Road in 1939.

TOLEDO SCALE AT THE FAIR

TOLEDO SCALE EXHIBIT

Taking a cue from Libbey's original success exhibiting his products in Chicago at the World's Columbian Exposition in 1893, several Toledo companies followed the practice. As shown in these postcards, Toledo Scale displayed its products at the St. Louis World's Fair in 1904 and the Panama-Pacific Exposition in San Francisco in 1915.

RUEDY'S MEAT MARKET

Toledo Scales, as they were commonly called, and their slogan, "No Springs, Honest Weight," became known the world over. This circa 1908 postcard of Ruedy's Meat Market, 1001 Cherry Street in Toledo, shows two fine examples of scales made by the Toledo Scale Company.

WILLYS-KNIGHT ADVERTISEMENT

In 1914 the new four-cylinder sleeve valve Willys-Knight model automobile was introduced. Many customers were impressed by its efficient and quiet performance. Between 1915 and 1940, Willys sold more mid-priced sleeve valve automobiles than all other car makers combined.* The adaptation of the sleeve valve engine was successful. Willys concentrated production efforts thereafter on just three main lines; the inexpensive Overlands, the mid-priced Knights, and a new Willys Six model.

* Figures suggest up to 50,000 per year, or nearly half a million in total.

THE TOLEDO TIMER COMPANY

FLYIN' HIGH

Toledo businesses provided many innovations and improvements in auto parts. The market for Toledo auto parts suppliers included the nearby Detroit vehicle makers as well as Willys-Overland. This advertising postcard by The Toledo Timer Company points out that they supplied timers to the Ford Motor Company. The notations on the postcard back outline the advantages and new features of their products.

FIRST SUCCESSFUL FLIGHT OF AIR SHIP, KNABENSHUE, KING OF THE AIR, IN FLIGHT FROM FAIR GROUNDS TO THE TOP OF THE SPITZER BLDG. JUNE 28, 1905, TOLEDO, O.

UNSUCCESSFUL FLIGHT

DIRIGIBLE IN FLIGHT

After his success piloting Captain Baldwin's balloon in the first-ever American powered dirigible flights at the St. Louis World's Fair in 1904, Roy Knabenshue returned to Toledo. He built his own improved dirigible which he called the Toledo I. It was a huge 58-foot-long canvas bag filled with highly flammable hydrogen gas. Netting was draped over the balloon and a wooden catwalk or gondola was attached underneath. A ten-horsepower gasoline engine and a small gasoline tank were bolted to the catwalk slightly in front of center to counterbalance the weight of the pilot, who stood a little to the rear. A rudder made of pipes covered with varnished silk was operated by the pilot via ropes attached to the sides of the catwalk. The pilot could make the balloon ascend by walking backward on the catwalk to raise the nose, and descend by walking forward to point the nose down. Maneuvering the Toledo I was a tricky and delicate job. This picture was taken on June 28, 1905 as Knabenshue prepared to make a historic flight from the Tri-State Fairgrounds at Dorr Street and Upton Avenue. He would attempt to land atop the Spitzer Building in downtown Toledo. Ironically the card was rushed to publication too soon. The flight on June 28 failed when the dirigible landed on the roof of a nearby house and had to be dragged off and carried back to the Fairgrounds by a crowd of neighbors.

KNABENSHUE ABOVE SPITZER BUILDING

On June 30, 1905, the craft attempted a second flight. Amazingly, Knabenshue succeeded in bringing the airship down to the small landing area on the roof of the Spitzer Building. The spectators had to help by pulling the ship down the final few feet with ropes. This was the first time a powered aircraft of any kind had purposely landed on a building. The feat was not duplicated for many years. Because of the publicity for the Spitzer Building, owner A. L. Spitzer rewarded Knabenshue with a $500 prize.

READY TO START

QUITE AN ACHIEVEMENT

This photograph was taken from the Spitzer Building roof just after Knabenshue left for his return to the Tri-State Fairgrounds. It gives the viewer a realization of the precarious and dangerous nature of these pioneering flights.

PASSENGER SHIP

In the years immediately following the Spitzer Building flight, Knabenshue barnstormed around the East giving demonstrations. They included a spectacular flight over Manhattan and a circling of the Flatiron Building—a feat that amazed literally hundreds of thousands of spectators in the streets. At the same time he continued to improve and perfect the equipment. On May 22, 1908, he unveiled a larger passenger version of the dirigible called the Jupiter. On that day he became one of the first pilots to take passengers in any powered aircraft.

THE DARING SYRIAN

NASSR'S AIR SHIP

Roy Knabenshue was not Toledo's only pioneer aviator. Anthony M. (Tony) Nassr, his contemporary and colleague, had witnessed a historic 1902 dirigible flight around the Eiffel Tower in Paris. When Nassr returned to Toledo, he built his own dirigible, and made many local flights. While not as spectacular as the landing on the Spitzer Building, Nassr's flights were technically the equal of any of Knabenshue's.

NASSR OVER TOLEDO

In this rare postcard, we see Nassr in his airship over downtown Toledo in 1910. While flying balloons all over the United States he gained notoriety as the "Daring Syrian." He became interested in heavier-than-air flight and became an instructor, training pilots in flying all types of aircraft. He served as the superintendent of Toledo's first airport located on Stickney Avenue, south of the Ten Mile Creek.*

Anthony M. (Tony) Nassr's father, Michael H. Nassr, moved to Toledo in 1881. His family was the first of Lebanese-Syrian descent to live in the city.

* For 140 years this stream was confusingly called both Ten Mile Creek and the Ottawa River. On October 13, 1961, the United States Board on Geographical Names designated the portion of the stream from Sylvania to its mouth at Maumee Bay, as the Ottawa River. The federal order specified that the tributaries continue to be known as Ten Mile Creek and the North Branch of Ten Mile Creek. Some confusion remains as Ten Mile is often spelled Tenmile.

VOICE RADIO BROADCAST

The first voice radio broadcast from building-to-building took place between Madison Avenue skyscrapers in Toledo. In order to demonstrate the technology, Toledoan Frank Butler rented a room on the top floor of the Ohio Building (Madison Avenue and Superior Street) and another room facing it on the top floor of the Nicholas Building (Madison Avenue and Huron Street). A transmitting tower was built on top of the Nicholas Building (large building center rear) while a heavy flagpole to suspend the receiving antenna was set up on the Ohio Building (with the Ohio Bank sign). Butler hired Toledoan Harvey Lucas to work with him and set up transmitting and receiving stations in the two rooms. On August 1, 1907, Lucas successfully sent voice messages from the Nicholas Building to Butler in the Ohio Building, accomplishing the historic first.

CHAPTER FIVE
THE DEVELOPMENT OF BUSINESS

For portions of the half century during which America led the charge into the industrial age, Toledo was one of the fastest growing cities in the country. Between 1880 and 1930, its population expanded nearly six times from about 50,000 to nearly 300,000. This unprecedented population growth created a huge demand for housing and all types of goods and services. A veritable explosion of commercial activity resulted. Opportunities to earn a living were abundant for anyone with the willingness to work. Thousands of businesses—both large and small—were started and most flourished as Toledo developed. Much of the retail business was concentrated downtown in a compact six-square-block area between Cherry and Washington streets and from the Maumee River to Michigan Street. Wholesale supply houses, markets, and warehouses supporting the retail trade predominated beyond the south edges of this core. Summit Street, Toledo's first commercial thoroughfare, flourished as the city's foremost retail location. In the 1880s and 1890s, most of the sizeable stores—Lamson's (1885), Lasalle's (1890), Tiedtke's (1893), and Milner's (1894)—joined the Lion Store which had been established there in 1857. Milner's, at the corner of Summit Street and Jefferson Avenue, was one of the largest and most innovative general department stores in the region. In 1929 the Milner building was sold to Sears, Roebuck and Company. It was the biggest Sears store building in the country. In addition to the department stores, Summit Street was packed with dozens of small retail stores and businesses. At times, crowds of shoppers had difficulty maneuvering on the sidewalks. Summit Street was also a primary parade route. Many postcards of circus elephants and military personnel on foot or horseback were printed.

Postcards document many similar stores and businesses spilling from Summit Street. Jackson Street, Adams Street, Jefferson Avenue, and Monroe Street filled in across St. Clair, Superior and Huron streets. Madison Avenue, cutting through the center of the downtown core, was destined to feature larger-scale structures giving Toledo its signature skyline.

When postcards appeared in the first years of the new century, a common theme was to showcase the incredibly busy street scenes and bustling activity. Also Toledo's finest hotels and lodging facilities were often displayed on postcards. They depicted a transportation-oriented city with many travelers enjoying the highest quality accommodations.

A popular use of the new and inexpensive postcard was advertising. Postcards often featured a storefront with the proud owners and their wares. Since a postcard could be purchased or made at the cost of about a penny and sent for a penny more, these views became one of the most effective and economical ways available to promote a business.

Looking at pictures of these businesses today allows us a glimpse back at the exciting and charged commercial atmosphere pervading Toledo at that time. The postcards convey a feeling of the aggressive and optimistic attitude toward earning a living in a city on the rise.

Intersection of St. Clair and Summit Streets, Toledo, Ohio.

LOOKING SOUTH

As downtown Toledo developed, certain areas became hubs for traffic. The earliest was along Summit Street where the city began. Later, after the Cherry Street Bridge opened, the five-point intersection of Summit, Cherry, and St. Clair streets became the busiest in town as all the traffic to and from the East Side passed there. This 1913 postcard is a panoramic view looking south from Cherry Street, down Summit Street on the left, with St. Clair Street bending in from the right. The Lyceum Theater is a block down St. Clair Street at the corner of Orange Street. Note the cobblestone paving, the trolley tracks and the monument to General James Steedman, Toledo's most famous Civil War officer.

INTERSECTION ST. CLAIR AND SUMMIT STS., SHOWING STEADMAN MONUMENT TOLEDO, OHIO

LOOKING NORTH

The statue of General James B. Steedman was commissioned by Toledo brewer James Finlay, in gratitude for Steedman's help early in his career. It was dedicated at the Summit, Cherry, and St. Clair streets intersection in 1887 and stayed at that location for more than 30 years. The intersection remained a heavy traffic area, as this post-card looking north on Summit Street from around 1918 shows. By that time, however, downtown development had shifted a few blocks south. Steedman's widow, who was much younger and survived the General by many years, became increasingly upset that the monument was not being properly maintained. In 1919 public toilets were installed at the site, prompting the statue's move to Riverside Park* where it stands today.

* Riverside Park was renamed Jamie Farr Park on July 5, 1988.

LOOKING WEST

This view of Cherry Street is seen from Summit Street looking west in 1910. Newcomer's Drug Store was a prominent fixture at this corner for many years. The tall steeple in the distance is St. Mary's (German) Catholic Church at Michigan Street. The large building with the square tower on the left is St. Francis de Sales Catholic Church at the corner of Superior Street. St. Francis de Sales is the only building in the photograph that remains today.

WALL-TO-WALL BUILDINGS

From the earliest days of the city, Summit Street was the major commercial thoroughfare. This view, taken around the turn of the twentieth century and looking north from Jefferson Avenue, captures the atmosphere of heavy commercial activity. The street is packed with a variety of stores and businesses, but there are no automobiles yet.

ELEPHANT WALK

As Toledo's grand promenade, Summit Street was often the venue for parades such as this one when the circus came to town. The photographer is at Milner's Department Store on Jefferson Avenue. The buildings behind the elephants are the Fort Industry Square Block.

THE LION STORE

Most of the city's major retailers were located on Summit Street. In 1857 F. Eaton & Company opened a dry goods* store there. The business continuously expanded over the years. While in England in the 1870s, Frederick Eaton purchased two large cast iron statues of male lions which he placed at the Summit Street entrance. The lions remained the store's signature—and a downtown landmark—for over a century. They can be seen on the sidewalk in this 1908 postcard view. The business was thereafter known as the Lion Store and generations of children sat on them at one time or another.

* Dry goods include textiles, ready-to-wear clothing, and notions, but not hardware or groceries.

LAMSON'S

Just down Summit Street from the Lion Dry Goods Company, the Lamson brothers founded their dry goods store at 159 Summit Street* near Adams Street in 1885. Lamson's remained at this location until a grand new emporium was erected at Jefferson Avenue and Huron Street, and opened in 1928. Postcards advertising the new store were not printed because the era of the postcard was approaching its end.

* The address changed in 1888 to 333 Summit Street. The City of Toledo adopted the Philadelphia decimal numbering system of number addresses in 1888 changing all Toledo addresses.

LASALLE'S

The Lasalle and Koch Company also started on Summit Street, occupying the new Bronson Building at Summit and Adams streets from 1890 to 1900. The store then moved to more commodious quarters in the Secor Building, the pink building on the left in this 1912 postcard view. This location on the northwest corner of Jefferson Avenue and Superior Street, catercornered to the fine Secor Hotel, was one of the busiest intersections downtown. Lasalle's eventually became one of the biggest department stores in the Midwest, and by 1916 it had outgrown the Secor Building.

49. LA SALLE AND KOCH BUILDING, TOLEDO, OHIO.

"NEW" LASALLE'S

In 1917 Lasalle and Koch moved into this massive new building at the southeast corner of Adams and Huron streets. On its grand opening day, an estimated 90,000 customers walked through the doors. In 1924 the R. H. Macy Company of New York purchased an interest in Lasalle and Koch and controlled the operation until the store finally closed in 1984.

THE BROTHERS AND OTHERS

Brothers Ernest and Charles Tiedtke started a small grocery store on Summit Street in 1893. Their tremendous work ethic, personal concern for their employees, creative sales techniques, and food sales to ships in port soon made their business successful. This circa 1908 postcard shows Ernest Tiedtke seated on the left and his brother Charles standing behind him with some of their employees.

TIEDTKE'S

As their business expanded, the Tiedtke brothers moved to larger quarters several times. They finally settled in this complex of store buildings on the corner of Summit and Adams streets in 1910. Tiedtke's developed innovative promotions and turned the store into a combination grocery, coffee house, bakery, fish market, and dry goods emporium with all manner of department store items. Tiedtke's provided a shopping experience featuring a pipe organ, distorting mirrors on the stairs, a huge wheel of cheese at Christmastime, along with the aromas of bread baking, coffee roasting, and fresh flowers. The store also delivered customers' purchases to their homes at no extra charge. Tiedtke's became Toledo's most loved store.

Milner's Department Store.   Toledo, Ohio.

MILNER'S

W. L. Milner established his Toledo dry goods business in this building at the corner of Jefferson Avenue and Summit Street in 1894. He enlarged the building twice, in 1903 and 1906, and it became the city's biggest store. Milner's became Toledo's first true department store with many different product lines under one roof. Innovations included the first electric escalator in Toledo and restrooms to encourage customers to stay in the building. Milner's remained in business until 1929.

CROWDED SIDEWALK

All the major streets in the heart of the city flourished with a myriad of stores and businesses, making downtown a beehive of commercial activity. Pedestrian traffic was often so dense that people had trouble negotiating their way along the sidewalks. This circa 1908 view at the S. H. Knox & Company 5 & 10¢ Store illustrates such a crowd. Knox opened this business at 319 Summit Street in 1894.

SUMMIT STREET

As the city continued to grow and develop into the 1920s, Summit Street maintained its predominant position as the major commercial location. This postcard published then shows Summit Street as an established shopping district at perhaps its peak. During these years, nearly 90 percent of the area's retail sales were made in downtown Toledo.

From the early years of the century through the 1920s, more than 300 postcard views of Toledo's streets were published. Sufficient postcards exist to create a virtual block-by-block walking tour of downtown. The following four postcards of St. Clair Street are examples of street scenes. The inclusion of many street scenes in the accompanying searchable compact disc allows readers to construct personal virtual street viewings.

NORTH FROM JACKSON STREET

SOUTH FROM JACKSON STREET

St. Clair Street was a major commercial artery during the first half of the twentieth century. This is a rare circa 1915 view of St. Clair Street, looking north from Jackson Street toward Cherry Street. The Lyceum Theater is down the block at Orange Street. Years later, the Lyceum became the Town Hall Burlesque Theater. The entire block was vacated for urban renewal in the late 1960s. This location is now occupied by the Community Services Building and the Vistula Parking Garage.

Turning around and looking south from the previous picture's vantage point, the St. Clair Street block from Jackson Street to Adams Street was dominated by the Valentine Building on the right. Also shown are several businesses and two popular theaters, the Arcade and the Empire. These, along with the Valentine, turned St. Clair Street into the city's theater—and later movie—district.

ST. CLAIR STREET AND MADISON AVENUE

The Produce Exchange Building, seen here on the right, was two blocks south from Jackson Street at the intersection of Madison Avenue. The famous Boody House hotel and the First Congregational Church were beyond Madison Avenue. In the 1880s this was the city's most prestigious corner. The new skyscrapers west on Madison Avenue were beginning to shift Toledo's financial center further from Summit Street and the river.

BOARD OF TRADE BUILDING

Moving one block south on St. Clair Street and looking back north, an observer a few years later would have had this view. As the twentieth century progressed, more and more automobiles appeared on downtown streets. Parking became an issue for the first time. The Richardson or Board of Trade Building was constructed at the corner of Jefferson Avenue and St. Clair Street in 1925. The building was a multi-level indoor parking garage disguised by rental space around the exterior and an attractive ornamental façade. The Board of Trade Building was an innovative solution to adapt to the changing conditions brought about by the advent of the automobile.

THE CALVIN BUILDING

Some of the most important and basic areas of commercial development involved supplying food products and other necessities to an increasing number of residents in the new urban setting. Neighborhoods had small specialty shops that sold meats or baked goods or other foodstuffs. As Toledo grew, the focus shifted to larger enterprises and wholesale operations selling these items. The Tiedtke brothers started as small grocers on Summit Street but expanded rapidly.

German immigrant entrepreneur Rudolph Bartley went even further, developing Toledo's most successful wholesale grocery supply house. Initially Bartley's headquarters was at the busiest downtown intersection, Summit and Cherry streets. Built in 1897 the Calvin Building, shown on the left, provided Bartley with office space. Warehouses occupied much of the block behind it down to the river.

BARTLEY WAREHOUSE FIRE

In 1908 Bartley suffered a devastating fire that gutted most of his warehouses. Much of his stock was destroyed. He relocated his operations to the south end of downtown on Washington Street.

SUPERIOR STREET MARKET

From the earliest days of the city, the neighborhood south of Monroe Street and extending to Swan Creek had served as the area of prime commercial activity. As the city center developed just to the north, this locality became a wholesale supply and market district supplying downtown. The covered market on Superior Street between Monroe and Washington streets had been designated a marketplace on Toledo's very first plat map. It remained a busy produce market where many residents and businesses obtained supplies well into the twentieth century. This market was set on the spot currently occupied by the playing surface of Fifth Third Field* baseball park.

* Since 2002, Fifth Third Field has been the home of the Toledo Mud Hens, the Triple-A affiliate of the Detroit Tigers.

NO PARKING SPACE

Wholesale supply warehouses filled Huron, Erie, and Ontario streets, from Monroe Street south to Lafayette Street, as shown on this 1910 postcard taken on Huron Street. Other than the horses, the scene in this block has not changed much in a century, except that the buildings to the right have now been replaced by the third base side of the Fifth Third Field baseball park.

CITY MARKET

The City Market was constructed by Toledo in 1908 at the intersection of South Erie and Lafayette streets. The building featured a stark and modernistic design of reinforced concrete and exposed arches with little decoration. Market stalls were offered to individual produce sellers. A 1928 addition called the Civic Auditorium accommodated flower and home shows, concerts, as well as small conventions. Parts of the building still exist a century later.

FOLGER'S PACKING PLANT

As the demand for food products grew, a number of enterprising suppliers and food processors developed major wholesale operations. For meats, especially pork products, the foremost business was established by Jacob Folger, a native of Bavaria. Folger arrived in Toledo in 1860 after a three-year butchering apprenticeship in New York City. He began his own business in Toledo in 1864 at the age of 20. As his butchering and sausage-making business grew, he concentrated on larger-scale production and wholesaling meat products for the retail trade. In 1883 he moved his meat processing operation to Phillips Avenue, adjacent to the railroad in West Toledo. There he built this packing plant. The Jacob Folger Packing Company became the largest wholesale meat dealer in the city. During its peak years in the 1920s and early 1930s, Folger's packinghouse produced three million pounds of sausage and bologna annually. The business continued in family hands until 1958.

BOODY HOUSE & FIRST CONGREGATIONAL CHURCH, TOLEDO, OHIO.

Lobby Hotel Boody

BOODY HOUSE

For many years the Boody House, built in 1872, was Toledo's finest hotel and best-known building. It was located at the very center of the city's developing downtown at the corner of Madison Avenue and St. Clair Street. It earned a reputation of being a first-class hotel and served as the venue for many of the city's elite social events. One of note was the Seventh Reunion of the Army of the Tennessee in October 1873. The most famous Union generals of the Civil War attended, including then President Ulysses S. Grant. At a grand reception for the ladies, a kissing contest ensued in which the generals vied to see who could kiss the most female guests. General Custer reportedly kissed the most ladies and General Sherman kissed the most babies. Another celebration at the Boody House was a mock wake held on the evening before the Prohibition Amendment went into effect in 1920. The decorations were black, musical offerings were dirges, and at midnight the guests threw their empty liquor bottles into a coffin.

SECOR HOTEL

By 1908 the Boody House was becoming dated because of improvements in architecture, construction methods, and building materials. Businessman Jay Secor commissioned a new hotel at Jefferson Avenue and Superior Street with 400 rooms, 300 of which had private bathrooms. The new hotel featured an elegant lobby with a large skylight, marble columns, expensive furnishings, and dining and meeting rooms. The Secor Hotel set a new standard for excellence and luxury in lodging in Toledo that continued into the late 1920s.

WALDORF HOTEL

Many other more modest hotels operated in downtown Toledo, including the Niagara at 324 Summit Street. The Niagara had an unusual and tragic history. In December 1900 it was destroyed by a spectacular fire. The building's walls collapsed and exploding window glass showered down on thousands of spectators. Shortly thereafter it was rebuilt, but burned again in 1915. Two guests died in this blaze. The following year it was replaced by the Waldorf Hotel. With ten stories and 500 rooms it was the city's largest hotel. It offered a full complement of services and was popular among business travelers. The Waldorf remained open until 1978.

COMMODORE PERRY HOTEL

The Commodore Perry Hotel opened in 1927 at the corner of Jefferson Avenue and Superior Street—at the same intersection as the Secor Hotel. The Commodore Perry became the city's premier lodging facility just before the era of industrial growth was brought to a halt by the Great Depression that began in 1929. The building featured four stories of elegant lounges with crystal chandeliers, a huge ballroom with ornate decorations in a Spanish theme, the exquisite Travertine Dining Room, and meeting rooms of various types and décor. The twin tower design provided natural light and air to all of the more than 500 guest rooms. At the time of its construction, the Commodore Perry was the largest hotel between Cleveland and Chicago.

Hillcrest Hotel, Toledo, Ohio

HILLCREST HOTEL

The last of Toledo's major hotels was the Hillcrest Arms Apartment Hotel, built in 1929 between downtown and the fashionable uptown residential district west of downtown. Located at Madison Avenue and 16th Street, its 245 one-, two-, and three-bedroom apartments were better suited for long-term occupants rather than for transients. The Hillcrest was converted into a conventional hotel during World War II. The hotel closed in 1990, suffered a fire in 1994, and was renovated into apartments in late 1998.

HENRY MILLER'S INN

Along with hotels, downtown Toledo boasted many restaurants and bars. City directories from the early years of the twentieth century list more than 600 saloons. A typical saloon was Henry Miller's Inn at 333 St. Clair Street, shown here in 1909. Note the boxes of cigars stacked behind the bar and the brass spittoons on the floor. The sign reads: "Oysters Stew Or Raw 10 cents." Mexican chili con carne is also offered for the same price. Drinks included Schmidt's Sweet Apple Cider, Pabst Blue Ribbon Beer, old English ale, and hot drinks of all kinds.

THE COURT INN

The Court Inn was on the northeast corner of Adams and Erie streets. Nearly a century after this postcard picture was made circa 1910, the building remains in use. The restaurant, bar, and inn was named due to its proximity to the county courthouse. The proprietor was Jule M. Surtman, who operated several bars and related establishments downtown at the time. St. Paul's Lutheran Church, another long-time downtown landmark, is in the rear.

GRADWOHL DELIVERY

George Gradwohl worked for Jacob Folger before establishing his own successful meat market, located at 408 Monroe Street near St. Clair Street. This postcard features George's younger brother, Clarence, in the Gradwohl Company's first delivery truck—one of the earliest motorized commercial vehicles in the city. The background in this 1910 photograph is Collingwood Boulevard*, near the lavish home of Rudolph Bartley, the largest wholesale marketer of groceries in Toledo. The Bartleys, Folgers, and Gradwohls were examples of small businesses expanding to meet the growing needs of a rapidly developing city.

* Collingwood Boulevard was Collingwood Avenue before 1937.

PECK'S DELIVERY TRUCK

This postcard from circa 1907 shows an early delivery truck—decorated appropriately with flowers—from Peck's Flower Store, located at 442 Summit Street near Jackson Street.

First Auto Funeral — July 28, 1911.
THE BOYER-KRUSE MORTUARY.
Monroe at Collingwood.   Toledo, Ohio.

FIRST MOTORIZED FUNERAL PROCESSION

The automobile brought about changes in the commercial world—even in the mortuary business. This interesting postcard, published by the Boyer-Kruse Mortuary at Monroe Street and Collingwood Boulevard, commemorates Toledo's first-ever motorized funeral procession in 1911.

THE AMALGAMATED GARAGE

As the number of automobiles grew, the need for service and maintenance became increasingly important. The establishment of filling stations and service garages followed. This circa 1911 photo postcard advertises The Amalgamated Garage on the East Side at 408-416 First Street. In 1911, automobiles were relatively new in Toledo and so Amalgamated was probably one of the first service garages in town. The proprietors, H. F. Menne, L. D. Walters, and F. J. Conrad, are posing in suits and ties. To be competitive, the garage stayed "open day and night."

MONKEY BUSINESS

This interesting circa 1910 postcard shows Henry A. Wersell's Pet Store, located in the Ecclestone Block at 506 Cherry Street, across from St. Francis de Sales Catholic Church. In the city directory of that year, Wersell advertises that he is an "aquarist and taxidermist, dealer in gold fish and aquarium supplies, dogs, pigeons, and all kinds of pets. Mounting of birds a specialty." In this picture, all the spectators—including the horse—seem to be enjoying the demonstration of the monkey sitting on the little boy's head. The pigeons are also prominently displayed, and the sign in the window offers parrots in a cage for five dollars.

SMITH'S CAFETERIA 513-515 MADISON, 2ND FLOOR E. H. CLOSE BUILDING. Seating Capacity 225.   Serves over One Thousand People Daily.

GRACE SMITH'S CAFETERIA

In 1916 Grace Smith opened Toledo's first cafeteria restaurant on the second floor of the E. H. Close Building at 513-515 Madison Avenue. The site was a poor location as customers had to climb stairs to reach the dining room. Nevertheless, Smith's Cafeteria was an immediate success. As this postcard proclaims, she served more than one thousand meals per day in her first year. Smith moved her operation to the new Bell Building in 1936, remaining there until 1971. Smith's was one of the most successful and fondly remembered restaurants in the city's history. Her dining establishment was a favorite of Duncan Hines. In its best years it served over a million meals annually. Grace Smith's reputation earned her the distinction of being elected president of the National Restaurant Association in 1941. She was the first woman to hold that high office.

CHAPTER SIX
A NEW CITY

In the 1870s and 1880s, Toledo's first major downtown buildings were constructed—the Boody House (1872), the Hall Block (1875)[1], the Produce Exchange (1878), and the Federal Building (1888). As the end of the century approached, wealth generated by industry and commerce provided the means for new construction. Urbanization and growth demanded more buildings. Modern technology and materials enabled construction on a monumental scale. A group of innovative young architects rebuilding Chicago after its catastrophic 1871 fire had been developing fresh concepts. They experimented with new materials and techniques to create highly functional buildings that soared into the sky. Supported by stronger and lighter steel frames, the structures featured fireproof materials, large glass windows, and terra cotta ornamentation.

Toledo applied the wealth, the need, and the cutting-edge architecture to build outstanding public buildings and ever-larger skyscrapers that included the tallest office building in Ohio. New neighborhoods with fine homes sprung up at the same time. The construction of core city buildings and residential developments mirrored the city's prosperity.

From the early 1890s until the Great Depression, building along Madison Avenue and the surrounding streets proceeded at a consistent and rapid pace. Toledo's tallest buildings rose during this time and transformed the city's skyline. The prospect of erecting the highest building promoted intense competition. For a time nearly every new skyscraper on Madison Avenue boasted more stories than its immediate predecessor. The Nasby Building had nine stories; the Spitzer Building, ten; the Ohio Building, 12; the Nicholas Building, 16; the Second National Bank Building, 22; and the Ohio Bank Building, 28. Madison Avenue was the home of the city's major

banks and financial institutions and became known as "The Wall Street of Toledo." Construction was particularly extensive during the prosperous years of the 1920s. The Great Depression ended the vigorous development of downtown Toledo.

In addition to Madison Avenue's high-rise office buildings, many commercial, government, and public buildings were erected in the city's center throughout this era. Taken in total, construction was a massive undertaking that reflected the size and quality of the community. Most of these buildings remain. Some—like the federal and county courthouses, The Safety Building, the Ohio Bell Telephone Building, the Toledo Blade Building, and The Toledo Club—function as originally intended. Others—such as The Lasalle and Koch Department Store, Lamson's Department Store, and the Commodore Perry Hotel—have been renovated for alternative uses. Still others—including the Board of Trade Building, the Waldorf Hotel, and the Paramount Theater—have been razed. A special case, The Valentine Office and Theater Building (1892-1895)[2], has been given new life. The theater has been restored and the offices have been converted into apartments.

The new captains of industry and business lived well. Fine neighborhoods were developed in what is now the Old West End, Westmoreland, and eventually Ottawa Hills. The first gated communities—Bronson Place and Birkhead Place—were established. Magnificent homes, rivaling the finest in the country, were built. The city's first multi-family dwellings were also constructed near the turn of the twentieth century. While development was centered in and around the heart of the city, the huge increase in population began to expand the settlement of neighborhoods outward in all directions.

---

1. The Hall Block was destroyed by fire in 1882.

2. The office portion was completed in 1892 and the adjoining theater in 1895. Together they appeared as a single structure.

The Old National Union Building,
Huron Street, Toledo, Ohio.

NATIONAL UNION BUILDING

Renowned Toledo architect Edward O. Fallis kept abreast of the latest trends. In 1891 he used a number of the fresh ideas to design the National Union Insurance Company Building on Huron Street between Adams Street and Madison Avenue. At seven stories, the National Union was Toledo's tallest edifice. It was the last and highest major downtown building entirely supported by masonry load-bearing walls. It contained 80 offices and a 1200-seat auditorium that served as a venue for shows and lectures. Well-known black poet Paul Lawrence Dunbar, who lived and worked in Toledo for many years, recited his work there. Toledoans had their first look at moving pictures in the National Union auditorium when Thomas Edison's kinetoscope* was demonstrated in 1894.

* A kinetoscope was an early motion-picture device in which the film passed behind a peep-hole for viewing by a single person.

8881. NASBY BUILDING, TOLEDO, OHIO.

THE NASBY BUILDING

The National Union Building began a trend of grander scale buildings. Fallis was about to take the next bold step, creating Toledo's first skyscraper. In 1891 Toledo pioneer and business tycoon Horace Walbridge asked Fallis to design a signature office building for the southwest corner of Madison Avenue and Huron Street. Walbridge wanted the building to be distinctive in style, to be eye-catching, and to reflect in some way the unique character of Toledo. Completed in stages between 1891 and 1895, the building reached nine stories. In addition, it was capped with an ornate tower and cupola which Fallis modeled after the Giraldo Tower in Seville, Spain. The Nasby Building was a transitional structure—combining established concepts with contemporary ideas. Traditional elements such as the splayed stone foundation supported the huge weight of the walls. It was adorned with ornamental details.* It incorporated modern elements including cast iron pipes to help support the walls, and triple bay windows to increase light and ventilation.

* See examples of ornamental details in the upcoming postcard titled Spitzer Building on page 81. A portion of the Nasby Building is shown on the left side of the card.

MADISON AVENUE

This early postcard view looking east on Madison Avenue from Ontario Street toward the river shows how the Nasby Building changed and dominated the skyline. Fallis was so pleased with his achievement that he moved his office into the tower suite and remained there until 1927. The Nasby project touched off a wave of competition on Madison Avenue to determine who could create the tallest structure.

Gardner Building,
Toledo, Ohio.

THE GARDNER BUILDING

Architect and developer Charles Gardner completed an ambitious and innovative building on his family home's site at the corner of Madison Avenue and Superior Street. Finished in late 1893, the seven-story Gardner Building was a copy of an Italian Renaissance villa in Florence, Italy. Progressive techniques and materials were utilized for the Gardner. It was one of the first large structures in the country to use concrete reinforced with steel. It is believed that Gardner's contractor bought used steel rails from the New York Central Railroad to add strength to the concrete walls. Glazed tiles covered all the floors and walls, making the Gardner the first completely fireproof building in Toledo. Another innovation was using concrete to cap the wooden pilings that supported the building in the swampy ground.

FIRST SKYSCRAPER?

In 1892, the year after the Nasby Building construction started, Spitzer cousins Adelbert and Celian began an ambitious office building diagonally across the street on the northeast corner of Madison Avenue and Huron Street. The financial panic of 1893 forced a construction delay, but the magnificent ten-story office tower was finally completed in 1896. It was such a success that the cousins built a large rear addition in 1900. The Spitzer Building was the Toledo's first skyscraper* with a complete structural steel frame. The innovation allowed construction on a larger scale. This postcard view illustrates the Spitzer dwarfing the all-masonry National Union Building seen directly behind it. Going forward, every new large building was supported by a steel frame.

* The Nasby Building is popularly referred to as Toledo's first skyscraper. By layman's definition and its impact on the city's skyline, it is the first. However, the architectural definition of a skyscraper is a building of exceptional height completely supported by a framework from which the walls are suspended, as opposed to a building supported by load-bearing walls. By this definition the Spitzer Building was Toledo's first skyscraper.

SPITZER BUILDING

The Spitzer Building was architecturally advanced in every respect. It used an artesian well* for an independent water supply. By far it was Toledo's largest commercial building with nearly 400 offices. It featured a retail arcade along an interior corridor on the lower level. The popular Spitzer Arcade was Toledo's first covered shopping mall. Beginning in 1917, a much-traveled passageway connected the Arcade to the adjoining Lasalle and Koch Company Department Store. This postcard photograph shows the Spitzer Building in the center with the Gardner Building on the right, and the department store behind. The Spitzer Building has been owned and operated continuously by the Spitzer family.

* An artesian well is one in which the water flows to the surface naturally because it is under pressure.

NICHOLAS BUILDING, TOLEDO, OHIO.

THE NICHOLAS BUILDING

Cincinnati unveiled the Ingalls Building, Ohio's tallest building at 15 stories in 1903. At that time Adelbert L. and Celian M. Spitzer were planning a second Toledo office tower and were inspired to make theirs even taller. As with many locations in downtown Toledo, the Nicholas Building site was swampy. To support the structure, it was necessary to install huge pine log caissons with steam-powered pile drivers. The Nicholas Building was named after the Spitzer cousins' grandfather. It was completed in early 1906 on the northwest corner of Madison Avenue and Huron Street, just across Huron Street from the Spitzer Building. At 17 stories, it became Ohio's tallest building. Because of its height, one of its first tenants was the U.S. Weather Service which placed weather monitoring equipment on the roof. The Nicholas had a large two-story lobby and atrium with a grand marble staircase to the mezzanine level. Like the Spitzer Building, it had retail shops off the lobby. With one thousand rooms, it raised the bar another notch in the drive for bigger office buildings. The Nicholas Building was long occupied by the First National Bank then became Fifth Third Center until 2008.

1544 OHIO BUILDING, TOLEDO, OHIO.

THE OHIO BUILDING

Businessmen began transforming the skyline and making Madison Avenue into "The Wall Street of Toledo." After the Nicholas Building was built in 1906, bankers were responsible for all of the remaining major buildings on Madison Avenue. The first was the Ohio Building completed in the same year. The Ohio Savings Bank and Trust Company's 12-story edifice was completed at the northeast corner of Superior Street. Conservative in style, it was covered with white glazed terra cotta tiles and a decorative frieze around the top of the second story depicting scenes from Ohio history. The Ohio Savings Bank and Trust Company was one of several Toledo banks forced to close as a result of the Great Depression. The Ohio Building was purchased by the Toledo Edison Company and became the main offices of the electric utility until 1971.

Perry's Flagship "Niagara" at Jefferson Ave. Dock, Toledo, Ohio.

SECOND NATIONAL BANK BUILDING

The Second National Bank Building was completed at the corner of Madison Avenue and Summit Street in early 1913. It was designed by the famous Chicago architectural firm of Daniel H. Burnham Company and built by the Toledo firm, A. Bentley and Sons Company. At 22 stories, it was Toledo's tallest building and the dominant feature of the downtown skyline until 1930. It was simple and functional in design, faced with brick, and decorated with glazed terra cotta. Here, it towers over the city during the centennial celebration of Commodore Oliver Hazard Perry's victory over the British in the Battle of Lake Erie. The Second National Bank merged with the Toledo Trust Company in 1924. The building was the Toledo Trust Company's headquarters from 1931 until 1981.

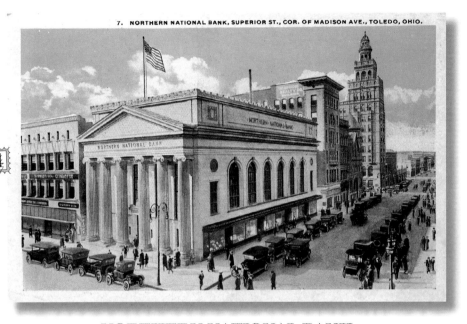

NORTHERN NATIONAL BANK

The Northern National Bank's Classical style office building opened in 1916 at the southwest corner of Madison Avenue and Superior Street. The space had been previously occupied by St. Paul's Methodist Church which moved west on Madison Avenue to 13th Street. It was designed in the form of a Classical Greek temple, a conservative style favored by many banks at that time. It featured retail stores at street level and large Renaissance style arched windows on the exposed Madison Avenue side. The building is presently occupied by KeyBank.

HOME BANK & TRUST COMPANY

The ten-story Home Bank and Trust Company Building was completed in 1924 at the southeast corner of Madison Avenue and Huron Street. The Renaissance Revival style building contained elegant offices and one of the most elaborate main banking rooms in the city. The structure was built around and over a huge vault in the basement. The bank's lobby retains its original beauty. In 1992 Mid Am Bank moved its headquarters here and subsequently merged with Sky Financial. Huntington Bank now occupies the building.

NEW OHIO BANK BUILDING, TOLEDO, OHIO

NEW OHIO BANK BUILDING

"The Ohio Building was the high point in the evolution of the skyscraper on Madison Avenue," wrote William Speck, Toledo architectural historian, of the 28-story giant that opened late in 1930. The Ohio Bank Building became the symbol of the city's achievement and transformation into a modern urban center. The grand office tower was 368 feet high, of contemporary design, and faced with limestone. The Ohio Savings Bank and Trust Company—the same financial institution that had built the Ohio Building in 1906—constructed the building but occupied it for less than a year. The institution was forced to close in August 1931 by the bank crash and resulting Great Depression. The Owens-Illinois Glass Company purchased the Ohio Bank Building in 1935 and occupied it until 1981. National City Bank, formerly Ohio Citizens Bank, now owns it. The building remained Toledo's tallest until 1969 when it was surpassed by the 30-story Fiberglas Tower.

DOWNTOWN SECTION SHOWING OHIO BANK BLDG. AND 2ND NATIONAL BANK BLDG., TOLEDO, O.   A-556

TOLEDO SKYLINE 1931

The gleaming white limestone of the massive new Ohio Bank Building contrasts markedly with the other soot-covered buildings in the heart of downtown. The Second National Bank Building, to the left, was superseded by the Ohio Bank Building as the dominant structure in the skyline.

MADISON AVENUE AND ST. CLAIR STREET, TOLEDO, OHIO.

MADISON AVENUE CIRCA 1925

This postcard, looking west on Madison Avenue and across St. Clair Street circa 1925, depicts Madison Avenue near the peak of its reign as "The Wall Street of Toledo."

U. S. POST OFFICE
TOLEDO, OHIO

CENTRAL POST OFFICE

In addition to banks and offices, Toledo began to build all the public and institutional buildings required of a modern city. A Central Post Office covering most of the city block bounded by 13th and 14th streets between Madison and Jefferson avenues was completed in 1911. The building featured a Classical style combining both Greek and Roman elements. It served the city as the main Post Office for nearly 50 years. One of the largest robberies in the history of the United States Postal Service occurred there on February 17, 1921. A local gang attacked postal workers unloading a mail truck at the 14th Street dock and stole more than one million dollars in Liberty Bonds, cash, and packages.

2003. Public Library, Toledo, O.

THE PUBLIC LIBRARY

During the 1880s nationally-recognized architect Henry Hobson Richardson designed many buildings in a heavy Romanesque Revival style, characterized by castle-like features and rough-cut stone. Richardson's work impressed several Toledo architects who utilized his concepts for many of the city's institutional buildings. The Public Library Building designed by Edward Fallis is one example. Erected on the southeast corner of Madison Avenue and Ontario Street in 1890, it remained in service for 50 years. It was replaced in 1940 by a much larger main library building on the site of the old Central High School on Michigan Street between Madison and Jefferson avenues.

LUCAS COUNTY ARMORY

The Lucas County Armory was built in 1892 in the heavy Romanesque Revival style at the corner of Constitution* and Spielbusch avenues. The building appeared, appropriately, to resemble a fortified castle with a heavy central tower and turrets as battlements. The Armory housed the Ohio National Guard, and hosted meetings and indoor sporting events. Adjacent to its south wall was Armory Park, the home of the Toledo Mud Hens from 1897 until 1909. The Armory was destroyed by fire in 1934. Fortunately, the fire did not detonate the large underground powder magazine, averting a major downtown disaster.

* This portion of Constitution Avenue was formerly Orange Street.

LUCAS COUNTY COURTHOUSE

As Toledo's population exploded, the 1853 county courthouse at Adams and Erie streets became inadequate. David L. Stine was commissioned to design a grand new courthouse to be centered in the entire block bounded by Adams, Michigan, Jackson and Erie streets. The completed courthouse opened to the public on New Year's Day in 1897 with 40,000 Toledoans attending the event. The site had originally been a frog pond. To commemorate Toledo's "Frogtown" heritage, Stine embedded a representation of a frog in mosaic tiles in the floor of the Adams Street entrance. The watery conditions caused the contractor such huge cost overruns that his company was forced into bankruptcy.

LUCAS COUNTY JAIL

In 1897 the county commissioners also constructed a Lucas County Jail, a residence for the sheriff, and the Lucas County Power Station to provide heat for the courthouse and jail as well as steam for the courthouse elevators. The steam tunnel between the jail and courthouse doubled as a passageway for prisoner transfer.

COPYRIGHT, 1906, BY F. W. WILKINSON
UNVEILING OF McKINLEY MONUMENT, TOLEDO, O., SEPT. 14, 1903

McKINLEY MONUMENT

President William McKinley was shot by an anarchist while attending the Pan-American Exposition in Buffalo, New York, and died on September 14, 1901. Toledoans were shocked by the tragedy and initiated a grass roots fundraising campaign for a monument to honor the late Ohioan. More than 26,000 people contributed to the fund, including children who gave pennies and nickels. Each donor received a certificate of appreciation. A complete list of contributors' names was buried in the granite base supporting the life-size bronze statue of the President. The unveiling took place during a grand ceremony along Adams Street in front of the Lucas County Courthouse on September 14, 1903. Lucas County was the first to erect a memorial statue to honor the martyred president and former congressman and governor.

COURTHOUSE NEIGHBORS

These three buildings, across Michigan Street from the Lucas County Courthouse, were all constructed during the first decade of the twentieth century. The tallest structure is the YMCA designed by Edward Fallis and completed in 1906. The building was one of the largest and best-equipped sports facilities in the country and housed the city's first indoor swimming pool. Bernard Becker designed the Elks Club which was completed in 1905, and is shown here to the right of the YMCA. Another Fallis architectural product and the first of these three to open, in 1903, is the National Union Building at the far right.

SAFETY BUILDING

Toledo has never had a dedicated city hall or a center for local government. For many years city offices for the mayor and city council were rented in the Valentine Building. Between 1916 and 1924, the City Planning Commission presented schemes for an impressive Civic Center Mall. The mall would become the center for local and federal government. A federal building, a safety building for city police operations, a city hall, and a county building with a jail would be contained in an area bounded by Jackson, Cherry, and Erie streets and Spielbusch Avenue. A municipal auditorium was proposed for Cherry Street, facing the county courthouse across the mall. Only the U.S. Court and Custom House on Spielbusch Avenue and the Safety Building on Erie Street were completed. Both of these stone buildings are of an elegant Classical style befitting their image and function. The Safety Building has housed the city's Police Division ever since its 1926 completion. The Safety Building also served by default as city hall until 1982.

12644   VIEW ON COLLINGWOOD AVE., NEAR BANCROFT ST., TOLEDO, OHIO.   COPR. DETROIT PUBLISHING CO.

COLLINGWOOD BOULEVARD

Toledo's wealthy residents demanded fine homes. Many of these were located in a neighborhood just west of downtown, now known as the Old West End. The Scottwood Addition was platted shortly after the Civil War by architect and developer Frank Scott. Scott, a son of pioneer businessman and visionary Jessup W. Scott, utilized family property for the venture. The area was bounded roughly by Detroit Avenue to the west, Monroe Street to the south, and Collingwood Boulevard to the east. Architect Scott was an early advocate of natural landscape design and laid out the neighborhood accordingly. The neighborhood featured broad streets lined with shade trees and spacious lots with homes raised above street level. Collingwood Boulevard, shown here in this 1910 postcard looking north from Bancroft Street, became the most prestigious of the Old West End's "wood" streets* and the location of many of the largest and most lavish homes.

* Other streets with "wood" names include Parkwood, Scottwood, Robinwood, Glenwood, Maplewood, Hollywood, Rosewood, Nesslewood, and Rockwood.

Residence of R. A. Bartley, 1,855, Collingwood Ave., Toledo, Ohio.
The Franklin, Toledo, Ohio. (England.)

BARTLEY MANSION

In 1905 the imposing French Renaissance style home of wholesale grocery magnate Rudolph A. Bartley was completed at 1855 Collingwood Boulevard. The massive three-story carved limestone building with a red Spanish tiled roof and widow's walk was criticized by some of his affluent neighbors for being overly extravagant. The home still stands, though isolated, at the corner of Jefferson Avenue and is a part of Museum Place.*

* Museum Place is a residential community located across Monroe Street from the Toledo Museum of Art in the Historic Old West End. Museum Place includes five renovated historic buildings in a park-like setting.

RES. A. L. SPITZER, TOLEDO, O.

2135

A.L. SPITZER HOME

This magnificent mansion at the corner of Madison Avenue and 19th Street was built for jeweler Henry Cook in 1879. It was later purchased by Adelbert L. Spitzer, who added the large wrap-around porch as shown on this 1905 postcard. The house had a huge third-floor ballroom which was the venue of legendary parties for Toledo's high society.

Home of E. D. Libbey.   (Libbey Cut Glass)

LIBBEY HOME

This 18-room home at 2008 Scottwood Avenue was designed by local architect David L. Stine for Edward Drummond and Florence Scott Libbey. Stine incorporated the colonial revival style in the three-story, 10,000-square-foot mansion. The exterior featured granite and shingles with a large wrap-around veranda. In 1895, after two years of construction, the Libbeys moved into their new home. Their only child William was born the same year but died 9 months later. The house was directly across Monroe Street from the Scott family properties that later became the site of the Toledo Museum of Art.

"Collingwood Avenue Presbyterian Church", Toledo, Ohio.

COLLINGWOOD PRESBYTERIAN CHURCH

As prosperous Toledoans moved into the residential area west of downtown, they financed houses of worship near their homes. Collingwood Boulevard became the "avenue of churches." One of the first was Collingwood Presbyterian Church, which opened this substantial and stately Gothic style building at 2108 Collingwood Boulevard at Floyd Street in 1905. This was followed by St. Mark's Episcopal Church (1906), First Congregational Church (1914), Collingwood Avenue Jewish Temple (1916), Second Church of Christ Scientist (1924), First Unitarian Church (1924), and First Baptist Church (1925-1930).

FIRST CONGREGATIONAL CHURCH

The new First Congregational Church at Collingwood Boulevard and Virginia Street was built during 1913-1914. The congregation is one of the oldest in Toledo and moved from its long-time downtown location on St. Clair Street. The building resembles the Pantheon in Rome and features a monumental portico. The interior is octagonal and seats 1,400 on the main floor and 850 in the balcony. Among the church's assets are a set of seven stained-glass windows by Louis Comfort Tiffany brought from the St. Clair Street church.

QUEEN OF THE HOLY ROSARY CATHEDRAL, TOLEDO, OHIO   1481

ROSARY CATHEDRAL

The crowning achievement of church construction on Collingwood Boulevard—and one of the most significant architectural statements ever made in Toledo—was Our Lady, Queen of the Most Holy Rosary Cathedral. Known simply as the Rosary Cathedral, the mother church of the Toledo Diocese was erected on Collingwood Boulevard at Islington Street. The major portion of the construction took place between 1925 and 1931. The Great Depression delayed some work and the intricate and detailed finishes required many years to complete. The church was finally dedicated in 1940. The granite and limestone structure, in Romanesque and early Gothic style, has many Spanish influences. A huge rose window* over the entrance depicts scenes from the life of the Virgin Mary. The Rosary Cathedral is an example of the accomplishments of a developing city, and one of the signatures of Toledo.

* A rose window is a circular window filled with architectural ornamental work often found in Gothic style churches.

Scottwood, Flat, Toledo, Ohio.

Published by Brown, Eager & Hull Co., Toledo, Ohio and Leipzig.

SCOTTWOOD FLAT

Toledo's first experiments with exclusive gated communities were Bronson Place (1899) and Birkhead Place (1904). Around the turn of the twentieth century, upscale subdivisions were created further west of town. Two of these—Westmoreland and Ottawa Hills—eventually competed with the Scottwood Addition in producing some of the area's finest residences. Housing for workers and their families sprang up around major factories and other places of employment.* Also during this time, developers began constructing the first multiple-family housing. One of the first such apartment complexes was the Scottwood Flat, which opened in 1903 at the corner of Monroe Street and Scottwood Avenue. Two other early major apartment developments were the Miltimore (1903) at Ashland Avenue and Winthrop Street near Scott High School and The Majestic (1907) on Cherry Street near St. Vincent's Hospital.

* Examples are Auburndale around the Milburn Wagon Works, Rossford around the Ford Plate Glass factory, Birmingham around the National Malleable Castings Plant, and Homeville and Homewood Park near the Overland factory.

BROADWAY AND SOUTH

Toledo's population expanded in all directions. The South Side experienced a large influx of new residents centered on Broadway. By the early 1920s, nearly a third of the city's total population lived there. Libbey High School opened to serve the neighborhood in 1923. The intersection of Broadway, looking south past South Avenue, is shown here.

POINT PLACE

Point Place developed to the north along Summit Street beyond the Toledo city limits in Washington Township. The community consisted of smaller dwellings, cottages, and boathouses along Maumee Bay and the Ottawa River. The permanent residents of the area remained strongly independent and resisted being taken into Toledo until January 1, 1937.

FRONT AND MAIN

The opening of the Cherry Street Bridge after the Civil War encouraged development on the East Side. Growth was accelerated after oil was discovered and industry began to arrive on that side of the river in the 1880s and 1890s. The population increased from about 5,000 in 1885 to 27,000 by 1910, and to nearly 50,000 just before the Great Depression. Main Street, extending from the Cherry Street Bridge to Starr Avenue, became a busy commercial center. In this circa 1918 view, looking east from Front Street, is the Weber Block—housing Leggett's Drug Store. The Weber Block has been a recognizable landmark for more than a century.

WEST TOLEDO

This postcard shows the West Toledo business section in the early 1920s. A substantial suburban neighborhood developed in West Toledo, focused around "The Point," where Lewis, Phillips, and Martha avenues meet Sylvania Avenue. The area became a busy hub for commerce with its own post office and a popular interurban stop for points west.

CHAPTER SEVEN
CHALLENGES AND THE PROGRESSIVE ERA

The population explosion that Toledo experienced on both sides of the turn of the twentieth century created demands for basic services. The municipal government provided a water supply, sewers, and fire and police protection. Private enterprise supplied other services, such as electricity, telephone, and distributing coal and ice. By the end of the first quarter of the twentieth century, most of the modern conveniences and comforts associated with domestic life were generally available.

The rapid growth of the city resulted in serious social problems. Crime, political corruption, mental illness, prostitution, labor unrest, and poverty claimed many victims. Addressing these difficult issues gave rise to a great social and political reform—the Progressive Movement of the 1890s through the 1920s. The movement was an effort to protect citizens by curing many of the ills of society. Proponents sought to install a more efficient municipal government, expand education, construct parks, improve working conditions, eliminate red-light districts, and promote public safety, social justice, and equality. Toledo's response to social challenges placed it at the forefront of the Progressive Era. Toledo produced significant leaders of the Progressive Movement—leaders who not only worked to address local problems, but also had an impact on the rest of the country.

In 1897 voters elected millionaire businessman and progressive radical maverick Samuel M. "Golden Rule" Jones as mayor. He worked tirelessly to improve working and living conditions and championed municipal ownership of utilities. With the help of Sylvanus P. Jermain, President of the Board of Park Commissioners, he developed a landmark parks and green space program which beautified the urban landscape and provided recreational and leisure opportunities for the public. Mayor Jones sided with working people and the poor against the established business interests. His efforts brought fame and notoriety to Toledo from all over the country.

Toledo was at the forefront in dealing with the social and political struggles of the Progressive Era. Mayor Jones and his elected successor, Brand Whitlock, left an important legacy in the history of American urban social development.

40. WOMANS BUILDING, FEDERATION OF WOMEN'S CLUB, CHERRY ST., TOLEDO, OHIO.

BRONSON HOME

The half century from about 1880 to 1930 was a time of great progress in technological innovation. Many of the elements and conveniences of modern domestic life became available. One of the most important advances was the arrival of indoor plumbing. In 1853 wealthy tobacco merchant Calvin Bronson built this early mansion away from downtown at 2920 Cherry Street. He hired a skilled pipe fitter to install heating pipes and washstands throughout the house. Rainwater was collected in cisterns on the roof and fed to the washstands by gravity. Most people could not afford similar luxury. The Toledo Women's Club purchased the home in 1911. This postcard picture was taken circa 1920.

3—Broadway and Waterworks, Toledo, Ohio.

STANDPIPE

Most Toledo residents obtained drinking water from wells until the 1920s. Both private and public wells were utilized. In 1850 Lyman Wheeler privately financed Toledo's first artesian well for his store at Monroe and St. Clair streets. Wheeler's venture was such an improvement over the shallow wells previously used that the city approved drilling four public wells in 1853. Three of these were along Summit Street—at Lagrange, Cherry, and Adams streets—and the fourth was at St. Clair and Washington streets. The wells were useful for people who lived nearby, but were not a long-term solution for a growing city.

Installation of a pumping station and distribution system followed in 1873, providing untreated Maumee River water primarily for fire protection. The water was not suitable for drinking.

The question of treating water had been discussed for a number of years and finally was addressed in 1902. The Water Works Commissioners appointed a Water Purification Commission to develop a plan. Their recommendations included using chemicals to purify water from the Maumee River. Construction of the filtration plant began in 1905 south of downtown between Broadway and the river. The nearly one million dollar facility opened in February 1910, providing the city with safe, good-quality drinking water. Following this paramount public health effort initiative, home plumbing became standard and the usage of wells diminished.

As the city grew and development moved farther away from the river, firefighters lost ready access to a water supply to fight fires. The city provided reservoirs at three public well sites for this purpose, but the supply was of little use for fires more than several blocks away. For the city to grow and progress, it became increasingly clear that a piped-water system was necessary. After several years of study, a committee recommended a standpipe*, gravity feed system. The voters approved a bond issue and the city's first pumping station and standpipe tower were completed in 1873, south of the city between Broadway and the Maumee River. The project included the installation of nine miles of water mains to which 50 hydrants were attached. By the turn of the century water lines had been built throughout the city and the plant's capacity reached 17 million gallons per day.

* A standpipe is a high vertical pipe or reservoir that is used to keep a uniform pressure in a water-supply system.

Spielbusch Fountain
Toledo, O.

SPIELBUSCH FOUNTAIN

John H. Spielbusch donated the majority of the funds to build this fountain at the corner of Cherry Street and Spielbusch Avenue in 1907. Spielbusch was the City of Toledo Treasurer at the time and intended the fountain to be a memorial to his father Henry Spielbusch. The elder Spielbusch was an early Toledo businessman for whom the street was named.* The fountain was supplied by a 305-foot-deep artesian well. It featured four drinking faucets—each supplied with two cups—and a trough for animals. The fountain remained in service until the mid-1960s.

* Spielbusch Avenue was previously known as Canal Bed as it was the former route of the Wabash and Erie Canal.

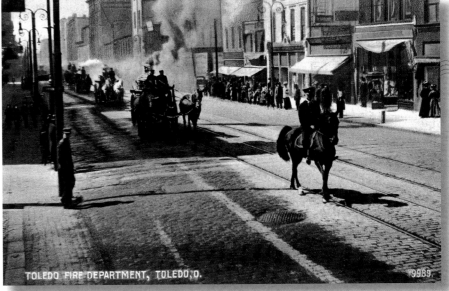

TOLEDO FIRE DEPARTMENT, TOLEDO, O.   9989.

FIREFIGHTERS ON PARADE

Fires caused fear and concern in early Toledo. In 1837, the year Toledo was incorporated, the City purchased fire-fighting equipment. Soon after, horses replaced manpower for moving heavy apparatus. Until after the Civil War, fire-fighting companies were comprised entirely of volunteers. Belfries of churches or schools were utilized to spot fires and sound alarms. St. Francis de Sales Catholic and Trinity Episcopal churches were both employed for these functions. After 1854 the clock/bell tower of Toledo High School on Michigan Street provided a vantage point farther west.

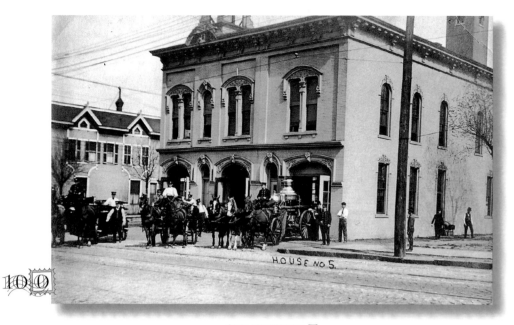

STATION 5

Following the Civil War, the volunteer fire brigades were supplemented by publicly-financed metropolitan fire forces. By 1880 the Toledo Fire Department was staffed completely by paid personnel. This postcard shows Station No. 5 at Broadway and Logan streets circa 1908. Strong horses were needed to pull the steam pumpers—the heaviest equipment in use. After 1873, water mains extended throughout the city, eliminating the need for cisterns or reservoirs. Before the 1920s, motorized fire trucks and equipment eliminated the problems associated with animal power. The motorized apparatus, along with electric alarm boxes, greatly reduced response times.

Toledo firefighters have always rendered courageous service to the community. Forty-five of them have made the supreme sacrifice. A postcard, showing the results of the R. A. Bartley Wholesale Grocer warehouse fire[1] in 1908, states that eight firemen and one policeman were injured. Fires have also caused huge monetary losses. The 1909 fire at the corner of Adams and Summit streets gutted the stores of the J. L. Hudson Company dry goods store and the Brown, Eager & Hull Company stationers, causing $325,000 in damages—more than eight million dollars in today's value.

1. See Chapter 5 for postcard of the Bartley warehouse fire.

AMERICAN THEATER FIRE

This dramatic postcard scene shows a 1911 conflagration at the American Theater* on Jefferson Avenue at Ontario Street. It was probably published for the spectacular scene and to promote the effectiveness of Toledo's Fire Department. The theater utilized heat from a furnace in the basement of a grocery store three doors away and advertised that there was no fire anywhere in the building—at least not until this blaze.

* The American Theater was formerly Burt's Theater. See Chapter 8 for details.

POLICE ON PARADE

Another of Toledo's obligations was to preserve public safety. Like the fire department, the police were volunteers until after the Civil War. The first metropolitan police force was organized in 1866, and it grew with the city, reaching more than 500 officers and staff by the 1920s.

TRAFFIC POLICE

As the number of automobiles increased in the twentieth century, police duties adapted to the new conditions—including the task of controlling traffic. Stationed at almost every intersection, traffic police began to appear in numerous downtown postcards. This is Officer Robert Bartley, keeping order with hand signals and good humor, at the intersection of Jefferson Avenue and St. Clair Street circa 1913.

Toledo's Motorcycle Police Squad

MOTORCYCLE POLICE

Toledo suffered its first automobile-related fatality when a girl riding a bicycle was struck and killed in May 1902. The incident prompted Toledo City Council to pass the first local speed limit law. Maximum speed was fixed at ten miles per hour. As more people drove cars, increased traffic caused dangerous conditions and the need for more law enforcement. Toledo's police department responded by forming a motorcycle squad, as shown on this circa 1915 postcard.

12649   PANORAMA OF WATER FRONT, TOLEDO, OHIO.

ELECTRICITY

The first practical use of electricity in Toledo was for trolley cars. Power was generated by the Community Traction Company's 1895 plant at the foot of Madison Avenue. The Toledo Railways and Light Company acquired the plant at the beginning of the twentieth century. It built lines to an increasing number of major customers including the Willys-Overland factory. In 1916 The Acme Power Company built a generating plant on Front Street downriver from the Cherry Street Bridge. Acme extended lines across the river to the Toledo Railways and Light Company to utilize its existing distribution network. By 1921 all these operations were consolidated into the Toledo Railways and Light Company. The company divested the trolley operations which reverted to a reorganized Community Traction Company. At the same time, it acquired most of the remaining electrical generation facilities in the city and renamed itself the Toledo Edison Company.

Central Union Float in King Wamba Carnival Parade, Toledo, Ohio, August 26, 1909.

BELL TELEPHONE

    The Bell Telephone Company installed Toledo's first telephone exchange in 1878. It later became the property of the Central Union Telephone Company which operated the exchange under the name of Ohio Bell. This postcard depicts Ohio Bell's float in Toledo's Wamba Carnival parade in 1909. It claimed to have served 10,000 Toledo customers by that time.

BOTH PHONES

    In 1902 an independent competitor—The Ohio State Telephone Company, known locally as the Toledo Home Telephone Company—challenged Bell's early monopoly by establishing an exchange of its own. Since the exchanges were entirely separate, customers of one company could not talk to customers of the other. Businesses had to subscribe to both services to ensure all their customers could reach them. The competition was finally resolved by a merger in 1922. The combined company took the name of the Ohio Bell Telephone Company. By the 1920s, as more and more people began to use telephones, the use of other forms of communication—most notably the postcard—declined markedly.

ICE DELIVERY

At the turn of the twentieth century, very few homes in Toledo were wired for electricity. Ice was used to preserve food in warm weather. Ice blocks were cut from lakes and streams and stored—packed in sawdust—until summer. Deliveries were made by a number of companies including The Toledo Ice Delivery Company. As most homes were heated by coal, ice companies balanced their work loads by delivering coal for furnaces in the winter months.

Samuel M. Jones, Toledo's Golden Rule Mayor, Born August 3rd, 1846 Died July 12th, 1904.

MAYOR JONES

Perhaps Mayor Jones' most important legacy and his most significant contribution to Toledo was his attempt to create a more egalitarian community characterized by equal political, economic, social, and civil rights for all people. Jones believed that the local industrialists and business leaders—backed by the government and the police and supported by the news media, the conservative clergy, and the prosperous citizens—were exploiting the common people. The progressive mayor went to war against the establishment.

observe the desperate condition of the poor in the crowded urban environment—a situation made even worse by the economic depression the country was enduring in 1893. Determined to fix these problems, he began paying a living wage at his new factory. In addition he gave a five percent bonus at Christmas, installed the eight-hour work day, granted paid vacations, lunches at cost, and offered day care for children as well as many other benefits that were ahead of their time. Instead of the typical long posted list of factory rules, Jones simply substituted a statement on treating others as one would wish to be treated—earning him the moniker of "Golden Rule" Jones.

In 1897 he embarked on a political career when he was elected Mayor of Toledo in a very close race as a compromise candidate on the Republican ticket. He soon surprised everyone with his radical ideas for social welfare and political reform. In his first address to city council, Jones proposed building municipally-owned artificial gas and electric plants. He advocated a new charter of self-government for Toledo, kindergartens in all public schools, a children's room in the public library, and free public baths. He also proposed to acquire more city parks and to create playgrounds for relieving some of the tensions of urban living.

Mayor Jones was constantly at odds with the establishment, but did not always prevail in disagreements. For example, his attempts to take utilities and transportation out of private hands so the city could regulate and operate them for the public benefit were all rebuffed by the corporate community. During Jones' tenure as mayor, city council repealed the Blue Laws—a major success for his administration. This allowed theaters to open, Mud Hens games to be played, and milk to be delivered on Sundays, among other things. This action raised the ire of virtually the entire city establishment. The business community, clergy, police and local government officials, and *The Toledo Blade* were all against him. Both political parties rejected Mayor Jones. Jones refused to play politics and never built up support for an Independent party. Therefore, he always had to fight an uphill battle against the council and powerful vested interests in the community. In 1899 he ran for reelection as an Independent and received 70 percent of the vote. He was fond of saying: "Everyone is against me but the people."

I claim no privilege for myself or for my children that I am not doing my utmost to secure for all others on equal terms.

Samuel M. Jones.

SAMUEL M. JONES
Mayor of Toledo 1898-1904

"GOLDEN RULE" JONES

Samuel M. "Golden Rule" Jones was elected Mayor of Toledo four times—with terms beginning in 1898, 1900, 1902, and 1904. He died in office on July 12, 1904, at the age of 58. Jones earned the "Golden Rule" nickname for the progressive management of his own company and the benefits he provided his employees. He advocated the same policies while serving in public office.

Samuel Milton Jones was foremost among the Toledo reformers of the Progressive Era. Jones was born in Wales in 1846 and immigrated to America three years later. As a child and youth he lived in near poverty. With little formal education, he worked in the oil fields of western Pennsylvania. Jones started his own oil firm in 1870. In 1885 his wife of ten years died and he moved to Lima, Ohio, to search for oil. He discovered oil and helped found the Ohio Oil Company. The sale of his company made him a wealthy man.

Jones moved to Toledo in 1892 and founded The Acme Sucker Rod[2] Company—a manufacturer of tools for the oil industry. He was shocked to

2. A sucker rod is part of the mechanical assembly of an oil field pumping system.

Ottawa Park, Toledo, Ohio.

OTTAWA PARK

NO.202. COR. UTAH & FASSETT ST. E.TOLEDO.O.

WOMAN BOARDING TROLLEY

One of Mayor Jones' most significant successes was the expansion of parks and green space. Jones was ably assisted by Parks Commissioner Sylvanus P. Jermain, a fellow visionary and an early advocate for parks. At the urging of Jermain, Ottawa Park became the site of the first municipal golf course west of New York City in 1899. The park and golf course are still in operation—more than a century later.

In an attempt to enforce discipline, Toledo Police Court Judge Lyman W. Wachenheimer proposed an ordinance to city council in 1901 that provided for "the arrest of men who stand on street corners and ogle women." The accompanying postcard view of the branch post office at Utah and Fassett streets in East Toledo illustrates Judge Wachenheimer's concern. The young men would have been in violation of the law had Judge Wachenheimer's ordinance been adopted.

While the "ogling" example affords a light-hearted diversion, the strict law-and-order views of Judge Wachenheimer and much of the Toledo community were no laughing matter for Mayor Jones. The Mayor had an opportunity to confront their differences directly as he sometimes filled in for Judge Wachenheimer in court. On those occasions, Jones infuriated the establishment by routinely acquitting almost all of the men arrested for vagrancy, drunkenness, rowdy behavior, and even some petty crimes. He said he couldn't punish someone for getting drunk and disorderly in a saloon while respected members of the business community were doing the same thing at The Toledo Club. Jones believed that the irreverent behavior of the laboring masses—their drunkenness and even some of their petty criminal acts—were reactions to being exploited and frustrated because of their powerlessness. His solutions to these problems were education and motivation rather than punishment and control.

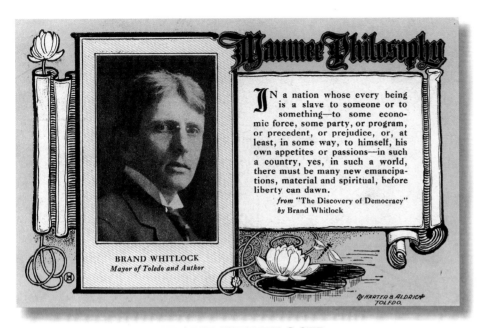

Maumee Philosophy

IN a nation whose every being is a slave to someone or to something—to some economic force, some party, or program, or precedent, or prejudice, or, at least, in some way, to himself, his own appetites or passions—in such a country, yes, in such a world, there must be many new emancipations, material and spiritual, before liberty can dawn.

from "The Discovery of Democracy" by Brand Whitlock

BRAND WHITLOCK
Mayor of Toledo and Author

BY KARTER & ALDRICH TOLEDO

BRAND WHITLOCK

Brand Whitlock settled in Toledo in 1897 and established a successful law practice. He was a friend and legal advisor to Mayor Samuel Jones. When Jones died in office in 1904, Whitlock assumed the Progressive mantel. Between 1905 and 1911 he was elected mayor of Toledo four times on an Independent ticket, but declined a fifth nomination. Mayor Whitlock continued Jones' reform efforts. In 1913 he was appointed as minister to Belgium by President Woodrow Wilson. Whitlock became the first ambassador to Belgium when the post was upgraded six years later. He continued to serve as ambassador until 1921. Whitlock gained international recognition for his success in organizing Belgian war relief.

For nearly two decades beginning in the twentieth century, Toledo became a laboratory of social experiments where conflicts between traditional social and political institutions and progressive ideals were played out before the nation. The example of the Progressive Era in Toledo and its advocates—Samuel "Golden Rule" Jones and Brand Whitlock—are still being studied in American social history classes at the college level.

St. Vincent Hospital. Toledo, Ohio

ST. VINCENT'S HOSPITAL

St. Vincent's, the city's first hospital, began in 1855 when four Grey Nuns from the Sisters of Charity of Montreal, Quebec, arrived to administer to the sick and care for orphans and the destitute. Health conditions were generally poor in swampy Toledo. A cholera epidemic had devastated the population the prior year. In 1876 the sisters opened this new hospital and orphanage on Cherry Street at a cost of $63,000. A bed in one of the common wards at that time cost 50 cents a day, but those who were unable to pay were accommodated without charge. A fire destroyed the interior of the wing that served as the orphanage in 1880. It was rebuilt and then replaced in 1907 by a separate building on the grounds. The new home for children was called the St. Anthony Orphanage.

TOLEDO HOSPITAL

In 1874 The Women's Christian Association purchased a home on 12th Street near Bancroft Street and established The City Hospital of Toledo. In 1876—presumably in response to the opening of the new Catholic St. Vincent's Hospital—its name was changed to The Protestant Hospital of Toledo. In 1893 the organization built this Romanesque style, 100-bed facility at Cherry and Sherman streets. The name was changed to The Toledo Hospital Association and then shortened to The Toledo Hospital in 1901. By the time this picture was taken around 1920, the hospital had built a large addition at the rear. In 1930 The Toledo Hospital moved into a 250-bed complex on North Cove Boulevard across from Ottawa Park.

Other medical facilities followed St. Vincent's Hospital and The Toledo Hospital. Riverside Hospital was founded in 1883 by members of the Women's Christian Temperance Union to aid unwed mothers. In 1906 Dr. William J. Gillette expanded a former clinic on Robinwood Avenue into Robinwood Hospital—an organization that evolved into St. Luke's Hospital. In 1910 the first section of Flower Hospital—a modest 28-bed facility called the Cinderella Carey Brown Memorial—opened on Cherry Street near Collingwood Boulevard. Finally, Mercy Hospital—the last major hospital facility to be established in Toledo before the Great Depression—opened in 1918 on Madison Avenue at 23rd Street following delays caused by World War I.

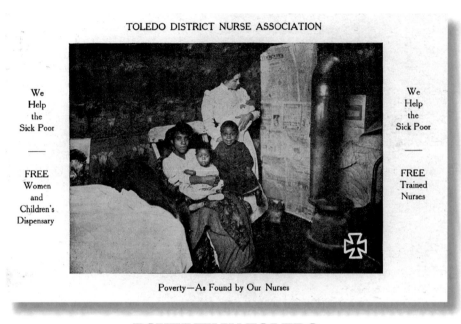

POVERTY IN TOLEDO

Thousands of people moved into Toledo from rural areas and foreign countries, creating some overcrowding and unsanitary conditions. These problems were often exacerbated by poverty and a lack of basic social and public health services. This postcard was issued by the Toledo District Nurse Association—a volunteer organization that provided medical and health care services to the poor.

Toledo State Hospital, Toledo, Ohio.

TOLEDO STATE HOSPITAL

Toledo can proudly claim that it was one of the most progressive providers for mental illness in the country. In 1883 the Ohio General Assembly created a commission charged with the task of locating a site for a new asylum for the insane. Representative Noah H. Swayne, Jr. of Toledo, chairman of the House Committee on Insane Asylums, was instrumental in forming the commission. Through his efforts and support from key members of the legislature as well as the governor, funding was approved for a new state asylum for the mentally ill. The facility was built on a 150-acre site donated to the State of Ohio by Lucas County at Arlington and Detroit avenues, about four miles south of the center of Toledo. Architect Edward O. Fallis assisted with the design of the complex. The project included 32 buildings, water lines from Toledo's Water Works Pumping Station on Broadway, steam and electric generating plants, natural gas lines, and the furniture, fixtures and equipment needed to accommodate more than one thousand residents. The first patients were admitted on January 6, 1888.

MEN'S COTTAGES

The Toledo Asylum for the Insane—renamed the Toledo State Hospital in 1894—was a radical departure from prior public hospitals of its type. Previously patients were housed in a central building. Instead the Toledo facility included 20 separate detached cottages as living quarters for all but the most seriously ill. "The 'cottage system,' as it became known, was conceived by General Roeliff Brinkerhoff, the founder of the Ohio State Archeological and Historical Society, who believed in abolishing the use of mechanical restraints in the treatment of the insane, and housing them in cottages to allow them the feelings of self-worth and independence while under the care of the state. The Mission Statement and Philosophy of the Asylum read, 'To many the subject of caring for the insane is…a mystery. The secret of their care and keeping them contented is to have them lead as normal a life as possible, with good clean, healthy surroundings, plenty of nourishing food, and fresh air.'"*

The new system proved to be superior to the traditional type of institutional facilities. The results for the patients were so successful that the Toledo State Hospital became a model for treating the mentally ill.

* Toledo Insane Asylum Drawings and Maps, MSS-221, The Ward M. Canaday Center, The University of Toledo Libraries.

FEMALE BUILDING

Patients at the Toledo State Hospital were granted as much freedom and as many privileges as their respective conditions would allow. Recreation, amusement, and useful employment were all considered means to help restore the mentally ill. The hospital provided entertainment including weekly dances to which the public was invited. Men performed landscaping duties, grounds maintenance, and vegetable gardening as well as excavated several small lakes to enhance the beauty of the setting. Women completed tasks such as sewing, weaving, and rug-making. Some of the patients stocked the lakes with fish.

MONROE SCHOOL

From the earliest days of the city, citizens were interested in providing education for youth. The first municipal board of education was elected in 1849. Compulsory education for all children up to age 14 was ordered in 1889. The Toledo Public Schools became the first district in Ohio to provide free textbooks in 1894. Dozens of elementary schools were built over the years to accommodate the rapidly-growing population. One example is the Monroe Elementary School at the corner of Monroe Street and Lawrence Avenue circa 1908, shown here. This school served from 1890 until 1965 when it was razed to make way for Interstate-75.

HIGH SCHOOLS

Toledo was in the forefront of the country's educational development in manual and technical training. The city erected its first high school building (insert of this postcard view) in 1853 on Michigan Street between Adams Street and Madison Avenue. Toledo High School was set on the site now occupied by the main library. This building served several generations of students and its clock/bell tower functioned as a fire watch location. The school itself caught fire in 1895 and was heavily damaged. The central portion of the building visible on this postcard was rebuilt in 1898 and the name was changed to Central High School. It continued as Toledo's only public high school until 1913.

In 1885 The Manual Training School for Boys was built adjacent to the Toledo High School—shown here as the large wing to the right near Adams Street. It was based on a model institution of practical training established by visionary Calvin M. Woodward of St. Louis, Missouri. The following year the Domestic Economy Department was established for girls. By making this practical training an integral part of the high school curriculum, Toledo became the first city in the country to provide free manual training for both boys and girls. The name and function of the former manual training site changed several times in succeeding years. It became Calvin Woodward Vocational High School in 1913, Woodward Junior High School in 1917, and Woodward Technical High School in 1919. It continued at that location as a junior and senior high school until 1927.

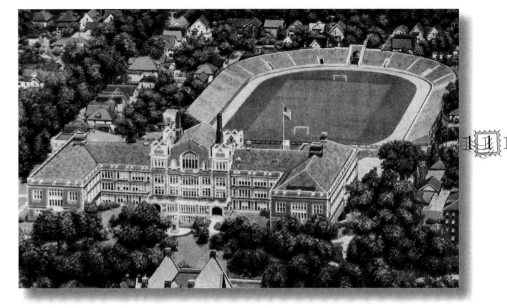

SCOTT HIGH SCHOOL

Central High School's enrollment grew rapidly and it became overcrowded a decade after it was rebuilt. The citizens approved a $500,000 bond issue to build two new high schools—one on the west side and one on the east side of the river. The West Side's Scott High School, on Collingwood Boulevard between Winthrop and Machen streets, was completed in 1913. Waite High School—using the identical architectural plan to reduce cost—opened a year later on the East Side, on Morrison Drive near Front Street. Both Scott and Waite built large football stadiums, and a great athletic rivalry developed. Thousands of Toledoans filled the stands for many epic Thanksgiving morning football clashes.

THOMAS A. DE VILBISS HIGH SCHOOL, TOLEDO, OHIO

1A3026

DEVILBISS HIGH SCHOOL

A fourth high school—Libbey—opened in 1923 at 1250 Western Avenue. A high school was provided for the North Side of the city with the construction of Woodward High School at 600 Streicher Street in 1928. With 215,000 square feet of floor space, Woodward is the largest school building ever constructed in Toledo and is the largest high school building in Ohio. As expansion continued further to the west, DeVilbiss High School was constructed at 3301 Upton Avenue in 1931, completing the public high school development program. Offering a parochial education, Central Catholic High School on Cherry Street was built in 1929.

TOLEDO UNIVERSITY, TOLEDO, OHIO

A-56

TOLEDO UNIVERSITY

In the 1920s the University of the City of Toledo was attracting students, but did not have a permanent campus. Classes were held in a former factory on Nebraska Avenue and in the old Illinois School on 11th Street. For a university aspiring to improve its standing, these buildings were inadequate. In 1928 the voters approved a $2.85-million bond issue to build new facilities for the university. The trustees then purchased an 80-acre farm and a 34-acre adjoining parcel on Bancroft Street and constructed University Hall, shown nearly completed in this 1931 postcard. It was the main building of the new University of the City of Toledo campus. At this time the Field House was constructed—and in spite of the difficult financial situation caused by the Great Depression—classes began in the new facility on February 10, 1931.

CHAPTER EIGHT
LEISURE AND THE ARTS

Toledo's prosperity between the depression that began in 1893 and the Crash of 1929 created leisure time for many of its residents. For many, work days were shortened and the weekend concept was born. Toledoans sought ways to enjoy the fruits of their labor and spend time away from the workplace or domestic duties.

As the city grew and became more congested, finding a quiet spot for recreation or relaxation became increasingly difficult. Preserving green spaces within the city became important. From the late 1880s to the late 1920s, Toledo acquired and developed 15 public parks on both banks of the Maumee River, totaling nearly 1,400 acres. The city constructed two golf courses, baseball diamonds, playgrounds, swimming pools, and tennis courts. Boating and yacht clubs were built near or as part of the park system. Three of the most popular parks featured proximity to the Maumee River—Walbridge Park in the south end and Riverside and Bay View parks on the north side. In 1895 Sylvanus P. Jermain persuaded city council to spend $100,000 for a 280-acre site over a half mile west of the city limits. This property was developed into Ottawa Park.

Sports—for spectators and participants—became popular in the later years of the nineteenth century. Prosperous Toledoans founded private golf clubs—The Toledo Country Club (1897) along the Maumee River and the Inverness Club (1903) west of the city on Dorr Street. Ottawa and Bay View parks featured public golf courses. Baseball came into its own as the national pastime and was popular in Toledo. Companies and institutions sponsored countless amateur teams. Professional baseball came to Toledo in 1883 and the game became firmly established when Charles J. Strobel built the city's first permanent ballpark in 1897. Armory Park, located downtown on Spielbusch Avenue where the Federal Courthouse now sets, was replaced in 1909 by the landmark Swayne Field—one of the country's finest stadia.

The popularity of Walbridge Park encouraged development of nearby entertainment attractions. An entire midway of privately-operated amusements and carnival rides developed along Broadway, just opposite the park grounds. The city also took the first steps to create what would eventually become one of the premier zoos in the country at Walbridge Park. The biggest of the outdoor entertainment attractions focused on the water—the Toledo Beach Company and the Lake Erie Park and Casino. Both of these venues were developed by trolley companies. The White City amusement park and The Farm, an upscale dinner theater, were started by entrepreneurs.

Early Toledo had a number of meeting rooms or halls for gatherings, lectures, and shows—many on the upper floors of commercial buildings along Summit Street. The city's first true theater built by businessman Jeff Wheeler in 1871 was the Wheeler Opera House at the northwest corner of St. Clair and Monroe streets. Designed in grand style, the Wheeler hosted many of the great acts of the latter nineteenth century before burning to the ground in a spectacular fire in 1893. The Wheeler was succeeded by the Valentine Theater at St. Clair and Adams streets, which opened in 1895. It remains one of the city's treasures over a century later.

The advent of electricity at the end of the nineteenth century created new entertainment options including moving pictures. Frank Burt, manager of the popular outdoor Casino, was the first to offer movies on a regular basis in Toledo. In 1898 Burt built a new theater, Burt's, at the southeast corner of Jefferson Avenue and Ontario Street, where it still stands.[1] By the 1920s most of Toledo's theaters, including the Valentine, had changed to showing moving pictures. St. Clair Street became a moving picture row with several theaters. The old First Congregational Church building, behind the

1. Burt's Theater was sold in 1908 and reopened as the American Music Hall, also known as the American Theater, in 1909.

Boody House, was converted into the Vita Temple Theater which showed Toledo's first sound movie in 1928. The culmination of Toledo's theater development came in 1929 with the opening of the Paramount Theater at Adams and Huron streets. The Paramount was the largest and most elaborate local theater ever built. Costing more than three million dollars, it was a veritable "movie palace" with marble and terra cotta finishes and sculptures. It hosted many of the top entertainers of the time.

The inception and subsequent development of the Toledo Museum of Art into one of the great institutions of its kind in the United States was due almost entirely to the efforts of Edward Drummond Libbey and his wife, Florence Scott Libbey. They desired that Toledo have a museum to serve as a cultural, social, and educational center. In addition, they wished the museum to benefit not only the wealthy, but all members of the community. Founded in 1901, its internationally known collections include representative paintings and sculptures by nearly every noteworthy artist and school, and perhaps the finest glass collection in the world. The Toledo Museum of Art became a true institution of, by, and for all Toledoans. Toledoans have contributed to the museum since its founding and, at the insistence of Edward Drummond Libbey, the institution was named for the people.

The nativity of the Toledo Museum of Art signaled a coming of age and a new status for the city. Museum Archivist Julie A. McMaster wrote of the birth of the Toledo Museum of Art, "A museum did more than bring culture to a community; it was a sign of status, and indication of a city's prosperity. In 1901, the citizens of Toledo created a museum that announced to all the world that their city had arrived."[2]

CITY PARK

In 1871 the City of Toledo purchased a private park from Peter Lenk at the south edge of town. Additional adjoining property was purchased from Horace Walbridge in 1873. The combined seven acres was at the northeast corner of the intersection of Nebraska Avenue and Elizabeth Street. The site was made into the first of many public recreation areas and named City Park.* Toledo's first park[+] was small, but due to its location in the midst of a densely populated neighborhood, it was immediately popular. City Park featured a tennis court and the first public swimming pool.

* City Park was renamed Rev. H. V. Savage Park circa 1997 in honor of the Reverend Harvey Savage, Sr. Reverend Savage was the founder of Lo-Salem Missionary Baptist Church and the Martin Luther King, Jr. Kitchen for the Poor.
+ Private parks existed before 1871. One of these was Lenk's Park which located on the City Park site. Perhaps the earliest private park was created when an area along the old Woodville Plank Road was platted in 1858 and a portion was designated as a "Village Green." Documented by historian and author Larry Michaels, the "Village Green" has since been made a part of the City of Toledo park system and is known as Prentice Park.

2. Julie A. McMaster. *The Enduring Legacy: A Pictorial History of the Toledo Museum of Art*, (Toledo, Ohio: Toledo Museum of Art, 2001), 9.

Pavilion, Navarre Park,   Toledo, Ohio.

NAVARRE PARK

Navarre Park was one of Toledo's earliest park acquisitions (1893). It was, and remains one of the city's most popular parks. It is located on the East Side near the home site of Peter Navarre (1790-1874)—its namesake. In 1807 he and his four brothers became the first permanent settlers in the area east of the Maumee River. Navarre was an experienced outdoorsman and had an understanding of Native Americans and their languages. His skills were valuable to General William Henry Harrison during the War of 1812. Navarre tracked movements of British and Indian troops and carried messages for Harrison. Many believe that it was Navarre who carried the legendary message from Captain Oliver Hazard Perry to Harrison following his victory in the Battle of Lake Erie—"We have met the enemy and they are ours." Besides this park, Navarre School and Navarre Avenue are named for him and September 9 is observed as Peter Navarre Day.

BOATING AT WALBRIDGE PARK, TOLEDO, O.

WALBRIDGE PARK

As the nineteenth century came to an end, Toledo acquired larger parcels of land and developed a number of major recreational areas—none of which was more popular than the 70-acre Walbridge Park. The park opened in 1888 in South Toledo along the Maumee River at its widest point, directly opposite Horseshoe and Clark's islands. The public immediately took to its large shade trees and high banks overlooking the wide river. Its desirability was also enhanced by the convenience of the Broadway trolley line running to it from downtown, as well as by its docks and facilities for bathing and boating. The Maumee River Yacht Club was also located at the park. A number of private concessions and amusement attractions developed along Broadway. Walbridge Park became the home of the city's fledgling zoo in 1900. From humble beginnings The Toledo Zoo developed into one of Toledo's major attractions. *

* For more details on a day at Walbridge Park, see Chapter 10.

12640   BOAT HOUSE, RIVERSIDE PARK, TOLEDO, OHIO.

RIVERSIDE PARK

In 1893 the city acquired an additional 63 acres along the river north of downtown. Riverside Park (now Jamie Farr Park) was developed on the land which extended from Galena to Ohio streets. Riverside also became popular and was a quiet and restful place with shade trees, gardens, a fountain, a large swimming pool, and a pavilion on the river. People flocked to Riverside on summer evenings to enjoy the breezes and watch the yachts and steamers passing up and down the Maumee River. As this circa 1906 photograph shows, Riverside Park was a good place for a drive. In 1921 the bronze statue of General James Steedman, which had stood downtown at the intersection of Cherry and Summit streets since 1887, was moved to the Galena Street end of Riverside Park. It remains there, facing downtown Toledo.

INVERNESS CLUB, TOLEDO, OHIO.

INVERNESS CLUB

Golf became increasingly popular in the early decades of the twentieth century. In addition to Toledo's public courses at Ottawa and Bay View parks, the private Toledo Country Club, founded in 1897, was developed along the Maumee River in South Toledo. The Inverness Club, established in 1903 west of the city along Dorr Street, became one of the premier clubs in the country. Inverness has hosted a number of major championships. This postcard shows the first—the United States Golf Association Open Championship of 1920.

AMATEUR BASEBALL

PROFESSIONAL BASEBALL

Toledoans have enjoyed baseball since before the Civil War. The city's first organized club was The Toledo Base Ball* Club which was playing intraclub games in 1860. The first City League of amateur clubs was formed in 1894. The Toledo sandlots have produced 30 major league players. Noteworthy from the era of this book are Roger Bresnahan, Frank Gilhooley, Sr., Fred Merkle, and George Mullin. Roger Bresnahan is the only native Toledoan to be inducted into the National Baseball Hall of Fame in Cooperstown, New York. During his 17-year major league career (1897-1915), he played every position on the field and was a manager. Later he was the majority owner of the Toledo Mud Hens (1916-1923). Gilhooley followed nine years in the major leagues (1911-1919) with a Hall of Fame career in the International League. Merkle was an outstanding National League first baseman for 14 seasons beginning in 1907. Mullin won 228 games, mostly for the Detroit Tigers, from 1902 to 1915.

* Baseball was initially two words—base ball.

Professional baseball was first played in Toledo in 1883. However, the sport was not legitimized as a business locally until Charles J. Strobel owned the team from 1897 until 1904. It was during Strobel's tenure that the Mud Hens' nickname was coined. Strobel's teams won pennants in 1896 and 1897, and he may have been the best manager that Toledo ever had. In 1902 he entered Toledo in the American Association, a premier minor league. Toledo remained in the league for more than a half century. The 1927 team, managed by Casey Stengel, won the pennant and went on to beat Buffalo in Toledo's only appearance in the Junior World Series. Noah H. Swayne was an ardent supporter of professional baseball in Toledo. He sat on the first team's board of directors and remained active in the management of the professional game until his death in 1922. Swayne purchased the land and leased it to the club for the building of a modern ballpark in 1909. Swayne Field was as fine a ballpark as any other in America and became the center for outdoor sports in Toledo.

This postcard photograph of the 1909 team was taken at Neil Park in Columbus, Ohio. This Mud Hen team finished sixth of the eight American Association teams, winning 80 games and losing 87.

THE CASINO

The Lake Erie Park and Casino was bigger than the midway across from Walbridge Park. Known as the Casino, it was located north of Toledo on Maumee Bay. As with Walbridge Park, the Casino was accessible by trolley. The Casino building shown in these two postcards, photographed just after the turn of the century, was a replacement built on the site in 1900—the original had burned down the year before. It was supported on pilings and reached by a 1,500-foot wooden boardwalk. The main building could accommodate more than 3,000 visitors. Octagonal-shaped wings were later added to provide space for refreshment stands, restaurants, and a dance hall. Other attractions were added when it was rebuilt—a roller coaster over the water, a midway with amusements along the shore, a German-style beer hall, and a small private zoo.

CROWDS AT THE CASINO

THE FARM

The Farm Theater—named for the barn-like appearance of its main building—was another form of outdoor/indoor entertainment. It was established by Louis Hanner on Collingwood Boulevard, near the Cherry Street intersection, and was a forerunner of the dinner theater concept in Toledo.

12. Shoot the Schutes. White City, Toledo, Ohio.

WHITE CITY

Capitalizing on the popularity of the amusement park, entrepreneurs in a number of major cities, including Toledo, developed entertainment complexes based on the theme of "White City." The name was borrowed from the great midway of the 1893 Columbian World's Exposition in Chicago where thousands of electric bulbs bathed the beautiful buildings in white light at night. Toledo's version was located on Auburn Avenue near the Ottawa River between Monroe Street and Central Avenue. The park opened in 1905. It boasted rides and amusements including the shoot-the-chutes* shown here. Picnic areas along the Ottawa River and a bandstand where Van Doren's Military Band performed regularly were other attractions. White City charged a ten-cent admission and had the key factor for success—convenient access for visitors from all over the city via the Long Belt trolley.

* Shoot-the-chutes is an amusement ride consisting of a steep incline down which boats slide into a pool at the bottom. Several variant spellings of chutes are found on postcards.

LOTUS BED ALONG TOLEDO BEACH R.R.

LOTUS BEDS

Trolley access led to the development of Toledo Beach in 1907. The Toledo, Ottawa Beach and Northern Railway purchased 254 acres of Lake Erie waterfront property in southeast Michigan, about 15 miles north of Toledo. The company named the property Toledo Beach to attract Toledo customers. A lakefront resort was built along with the company's new electric rail line. The line began at the Casino and followed the lakeshore to the resort. It passed through scenic marshes filled with lotus plants, water lilies, and various forms of wildlife. Interurban cars left downtown Toledo every half hour on weekdays and every ten minutes on Sunday. Groups could also charter a car for outings. On July 4, 1907, the first holiday after Toledo Beach opened, 14,000 visitors rode the trolleys to the resort.

TOLEDO BEACH

Arriving at Toledo Beach, visitors were greeted by nearly two miles of sandy beaches, a bathhouse for changing, piers, and a tall shoot-the-chutes. This 1910 post-card view was taken from the top of the slide.

BEACH PROMENADE

The Toledo Beach facility was beautifully landscaped. Nearly four miles of scenic waterways were installed to accommodate canoes and small rowboats. Picnic areas and shelters were placed throughout the grounds. Tennis courts, a roller skating area, a campground, a merry-go-round, and a baseball diamond were constructed. A restaurant/café was opened that offered hot lunches for 25 cents and refreshments were available at concession stands. A distinctive round dance hall with open sides was built. Band concerts and other entertainment were presented on summer evenings—the last trolleys back to Toledo departed at 11:00 p.m.

BEACH CROWD

Toledo Beach soon became popular—so popular that the Casino closed its doors after it burned for a second time in 1910. As this 1911 postcard shows, the beach was often crowded. The resort remained an attractive destination for as long as the electric trolley was the primary form of transportation. As automobiles became commonplace, there was more opportunity to experience other venues further from home. The popularity of Toledo Beach waned. By 1927 the number of customers on the Toledo Beach electric line had declined so drastically that service was discontinued. That stoppage, combined with the Great Depression, forced the closing of Toledo Beach.

THEATER DISTRICT

Many of Toledo's recreational and entertainment attractions of a century ago—including the theaters—were at least partially outdoors. There were indoor theaters as well. Among them were the Valentine on the left and the Empire and Arcade theaters on the right in this 1909 postcard view of St. Clair Street. Before air conditioning, indoor shows could not be staged in warm weather, and so the indoor theater season began in the fall.

LYCEUM THEATER

Toledo's first theater was the 1,400-seat Wheeler Opera House at the northwest corner of Monroe and St. Clair streets. The Wheeler was state-of-the-art for its time and served Toledo well. It presented the leading performers of the day including Sarah Bernhardt and Joseph Jefferson. Despite many precautions against fire—including 350 barrels of water stored on the roof—it burned to the ground early in the morning of March 17, 1893. When the Wheeler burned, much of the theater business moved to the New People's Theater in this building five blocks down St. Clair Street at Orange Street. The building was formerly a pork-packing house. It was remodeled into an 1,800-seat theater in 1885 by local impresario Sam Brady. The theater featured vaudeville and family shows, which were unfailingly clean and wholesome. Their quality, however, was clearly a step below the headline acts, top operas, and plays of the time. When the Valentine opened just up the street in 1895, and Brady experienced increasing competition from other new competitors—including from the powerful Whitney chain of theaters based in Detroit—he was forced to sell. The new owners changed the name to the Lyceum Theater in 1899, as shown in this 1912 postcard view.

THE VALENTINE BUILDING

In 1892 prominent Toledo businessman and breeder of champion horses, George H. Ketcham, planned to build a grand new opera house on his property at the northwest corner of Adams and St. Clair streets. Ubiquitous architect Edward Fallis designed the simple and elegant four-story Renaissance style structure. It included retail stores on the ground floor along both street frontages and offices on the entire second floor to be occupied by the city government. But the crowning glory of the new Valentine Building—named for Valentine B. Ketcham, the developer's father, who a few years earlier had become Toledo's first millionaire—was the theater. Opening in 1895, the theater was hailed as one of the finest between New York and Chicago. It seated 1,900 people among the elegant finishes. The theater utilized the latest developments in fireproof materials and technology, including exhaust fans in the roof and a heavy asbestos curtain to isolate the stage from the audience. The potential for fire was minimized by a system of all-electric lighting—with 2,500 bulbs and the ability to create special theatrical lighting effects. Electricity was provided by seven generators in the basement.

For the next couple of decades the Valentine and other smaller theaters in downtown Toledo benefited from the city's advantageous location on the main rail route from the Atlantic seaboard to Chicago. All the important entertainers and shows of the time stopped in Toledo allowing theater-goers to enjoy first-rate entertainment. Eventually, however, technology advanced to the point where moving pictures overtook the live theater. In 1917 the Valentine Theater was converted to a movie house. All the other theaters in town soon made the same transformation. In 1928 the advent of sound movies gave a huge boost to the motion picture industry. That year the Vita Temple Theater screened Al Jolson in *The Singing Fool* as Toledo's first sound movie showing.

29   TOLEDO PARAMOUNT THEATRE, TOLEDO, OHIO

4297-29

THE PARAMOUNT THEATER

With the opening of the Paramount Theater on Adams and Huron streets in 1929, Toledo boasted the ultimate grand movie palace. With 3,400 seats, the $3,000,000 Paramount was the largest and most elaborate theater ever built in Toledo. The building featured marble, terrazzo, gilded plaster relief, chandeliers, silk and brocade, and the most expensive furnishings. The elaborate main auditorium was designed to resemble an outdoor courtyard. The ceiling was made of painted canvas to mimic the sky. Lights created the effects of any time of day or stars at night. Cool water from what remained of the downtown swamp deep under the basement was pumped and utilized to make the Paramount the first air-conditioned building in Toledo. The Paramount became the city's main entertainment venue over the next three decades. However, its construction cost and the burdens of operating and maintaining it were too great for it to be profitable over the long term. By the 1950s television caused the next revolution in viewing habits, heralding the beginning of the end for the Paramount. It closed and the building was demolished in 1965.

Toledo Museum of Art. Toledo, Ohio

MUSEUM HOUSE

At its founding in 1901 the Toledo Museum of Art did not own any art or a building. For the first year it rented rooms in the Gardner Building and exhibited loaned works of art. In 1902 Edward Drummond Libbey renovated this former home on Madison Avenue and 13th Street. He added the wings shown on this 1905 postcard. He then leased the building to the Museum Association to serve as the new headquarters and gallery for the museum. In 1903 the organization retained George W. Stevens, a newspaperman, poet, and artist, to be the museum's director. His wife, Nina Spalding Stevens, was appointed assistant director.

STEELINK'S SHEEP

According to Nina Stevens, at the time the museum occupied the house, its entire collection consisted of this painting of sheep by little-known Dutch artist Wilm Steelink, a mummified cat, a table in the office, and a few chairs. Paintings and other works of art were donated. Edward and Florence Libbey traveled to Egypt in the winter of 1905-1906. They sent back hundreds of archaeological artifacts and two mummies. A few years later Florence Libbey established the Maurice Scott Gallery in honor of her father and donated several American paintings for display. Edward Libbey also started and helped develop a glass collection, aiming to show the development of glassmaking from ancient times. Over time a number of wealthy Toledo patrons donated their private collections. When Edward Drummond Libbey died in 1925 his personal collection was given to the museum.

From its inception, the Toledo Museum of Art was a pioneer in making art accessible to all. Edward Libbey first proposed the revolutionary idea that the museum should be open to the public free of charge every day of the year. Libbey and Director Stevens also promoted free education in the arts for Toledo's school children. By 1908 the museum had established training classes for some 5,000 children—a program many other museums in the country sought to copy. Since then generations of Toledo children have benefited from courses and training in painting, sculpture, photography, design, music history, theory and appreciation, and many other areas.

MUSEUM UNDER CONSTRUCTION

By 1908 the museum had filled the Madison Avenue mansion to capacity. Edward Drummond Libbey announced he would pledge $105,000 toward the construction of a permanent museum building if the community would raise $50,000. The people contributed that amount in less than a month. The participation and enthusiasm of the public encouraged Libbey to also give works of art from his personal collection. Florence Libbey donated the land on Monroe Street which included her father's former home. The new building was constructed in understated classical Greek style and dedicated on January 17, 1912. It was an immediate success. Memberships grew to more than 2,000 and the annual attendance was about 100,000 in 1913 and 1914. By 1925 more Libbey gifts and community support led to an addition in the rear doubling the size. Unfortunately, Mr. Libbey died a few months before the addition was completed and Director Stevens died less than a year later. Libbey left the museum generously endowed by any standard. Attendance, which had been 15,000 in 1903, grew to more than 150,000 in 1926. The public's support made it one of the great and enduring cultural assets of the community.

SCULPTURE GALLERY

This circa 1915 postcard depicts the central court of the museum building soon after it was completed. Many of the sculptures were reproductions or cast copies of famous bronze works. Some were purchased by Florence Scott Libbey as part of a study collection for art students. Education was always in the minds of the founders and programs evolved to train countless students over the years.

TOLEDO ART MUSEUM. TOLEDO. OHIO   A-565

MUSEUM EXPANSION

Even as the south addition to the museum's central building opened in 1926, trustees were planning for further growth in the form of two large wings on the east and west. Libbey had left money in his estate for future expansion in the form of a life trust to his wife Florence. In 1930 the Great Depression had left so many Toledoans unemployed that she renounced her interest in the funds to allow the museum to start building. She desired that "work might proceed at a time when the expenditure of a large sum of money would do the greatest economic good."* The construction employed 2,500 men for two years. This postcard view was taken in 1933 just after the much-appreciated project was finished. The west wing contained galleries and the cloister on the main floor, and studios and classrooms for art students below. The east wing contained a gallery, spaces for classical art, and the 1,710-seat Peristyle auditorium.

* The Toledo Museum of Art. *Selections From The Toledo Museum of Art* (New York: Hudson Hills Press, 1995), 24.

THE PERISTYLE

At Florence Libbey's request the Peristyle was designed to resemble a classical outdoor amphitheater. Also encouraged by Mrs. Libbey's interests, the museum assumed a leading role—unusual for visual art institutions at the time—to promote music and music education. The Peristyle has served as the home of the Toledo Symphony Orchestra since 1943. Over the years the museum has continued to grow and is recognized as one of the finest art institutions in the nation. It has enriched the social and cultural lives of countless Toledoans and is an asset that gives Toledo its distinct character.

CHAPTER NINE

THE NATIONAL SPOTLIGHT

Toledo hosted a number of important events in the early decades of the twentieth century that focused national and international attention on the city. This chapter is devoted to three of these—the 42nd National Encampment of the Grand Army of the Republic in 1908, the Wamba Carnival in 1909, and the world heavyweight boxing championship fight between Jack Dempsey and Jess Willard in 1919. All of these occasions drew thousands of visitors to Toledo and helped promote the city in new ways. As major spectacles, and because of their timing, these happenings also generated many picture postcards. They help recapture some of the atmosphere and dynamic social impact of these events.

42nd National Encampment of the Grand Army of the Republic

The largest gathering ever assembled in Toledo took place from August 31 to September 5, 1908. Nearly 100,000 members of the Grand Army of the Republic (GAR)—Union military veterans of the Civil War and their families—converged on the city. Veterans arrived from all over the country to participate in the group's 42nd annual Encampment since the end of the war. The GAR was a fraternal organization formed in July 1866. Its purpose was to assist veterans in obtaining pensions, to establish soldiers' homes, and to care for veterans' widows and orphans. Another objective of the GAR was to honor the valor and sacrifice of those who gave their lives to preserve the Union. To promote the latter, the GAR initiated and helped establish the observation of Memorial Day.*

* The original name was Decoration Day. Memorial Day was first used in 1882. It did not become more common until after World War II and was not declared the official name by Federal law until 1967.

WELCOME

TOLEDO VETERANS

The first Toledo chapter, or Post, of the GAR was established in November 1866—just after the organization's founding on April 6, 1866. It was named Forsyth Post after Lieutenant George Duncan Forsyth, a Northwest Ohio native who served bravely in the 100th Ohio Volunteer Infantry. He was captured in Tennessee and sent to Libby Prison in Richmond, Virginia, where he was shot and killed by one of the prison guards in 1863. His remains were brought back to Toledo and buried in Forest Cemetery. This postcard shows the surviving local veterans of the Forsyth Post at the Toledo Reunion in 1908 posing at the Lucas County Courthouse. Dressed in their Union blue uniforms, they are ready to participate in the upcoming grand parade and review on September 2. The men carry on their shoulders a frame displaying the unit's shield and motto, "We All Drink From The Same Canteen."

60-FOOT FLAGS

Both the City of Toledo and Lucas County appropriated generous budgets for decorating public buildings and streets with flags and buntings in red, white, and blue. Business owners followed suit and event organizers enlisted individuals and homeowners to catch the spirit. The national organization also provided three spectacular flag signs, each illuminated by 550 red, white, and blue electric bulbs. The local Citizens' Committee in charge of organizing for the Encampment proclaimed that the streets were "a blaze of glory after dark and a wealth of color by day."* Total expenditures for the decorations—estimated to weigh 75 tons—exceeded $50,000.

* Grand Army of the Republic. National Encampment. (42d:1908 Toledo, Ohio).Citizens' Committee. *Official souvenir forty-second National Encampment, Grand Army of the Republic August thirty-first to September fifth, Toledo, Ohio, 1908,* (Toledo, Ohio: The Franklin Printing & Engraving Co., 1908), 29.

NEWSBOYS IN GAR PARADE

The Toledo Newsboys performed valuable services throughout the week of the Encampment. As shown here, their impressive band of 50 members participated in the grand parade. Nearly 500 of them were organized and trained by their founder John Gunckel and by their officers to serve as guides and helpers for visitors. They were praised by the city's guests for being unfailingly courteous and became unexpected ambassadors of goodwill for Toledo.

LINCOLN FUNERAL CAR

During the Encampment, the Lamson brothers, owners of Lamson's Department Store, issued a souvenir postcard reproducing a rare family photograph of the Lincoln funeral car. Their father Myron H. Lamson, a mechanic, had helped to refit the railroad car used to transport the body of the martyred President to his final resting place in Illinois. A free copy of the card was offered to everyone who visited their store during the week of the Encampment. The Lamsons explained the story and their motivation in a printed message on the back: "Now that a united nation reveres the memory of Lincoln and everything connected with his life and death, we thought it appropriate that we should present this picture to the brave men to whom our nation is so greatly indebted." The Lamsons claimed to have printed 300,000 of these cards. Those which survived the century since have become valuable memorabilia for Lincoln collectors and deltiologists.

DELEGATIONS ARRIVE

The various delegations began to arrive on Monday, August 31. Most traveled by train into the Union Station. Entire units that arrived together were met by officials at the depot. Those units were escorted to their lodgings as shown on this postcard view along Summit Street. Some came from nearby towns on the many electric railways servicing Toledo and others came by boat. As the picture shows, the visitors were greeted with warmth and enthusiasm by the local residents. The organizing committee had calculated that accommodations would be needed for nearly 100,000 guests. Most were housed in private homes since all the hotels, meeting halls, schools, and other public buildings could only handle about a third of the expected total. The grounds of the White City amusement park on Auburn Avenue near the Ottawa River were turned into a tent city, accommodating about 5,000 people. Many Toledo residents volunteered to help during the event, and others invited the veterans into their homes.

CIVIC PARADE

On Tuesday morning, September 1, the city entertained the huge crowd of new arrivals with a civic parade. Participants included policemen, firemen, and other uniformed public workers. The marchers contributed to the overall proceedings as they were not paid for their time away from work. At 2:00 p.m. the scene shifted to Fort Meigs in Perrysburg, Ohio where the monument to the heroes of the War of 1812 was dedicated. Many dignitaries and about 3,000 veterans attended the ceremony.

FORSYTH POST ON PARADE

LIVING FLAG

The highlight of the week was the grand parade and review of the veterans on Wednesday morning, September 2. Nearly 25,000 marchers, averaging 67 years of age, participated. The route was nearly two and a half miles long. Though nearly three and a half hours were required for the entire contingent to pass by any given point, surprisingly few of the elderly marchers dropped out due to fatigue or illness. The veterans were mustered for the march along Madison Avenue near 15th Street. During the tedious process of organizing the various units in order, local women's groups and volunteers served 25,000 sandwiches and cups of coffee. Alvin Woolson, himself a Civil War veteran, of Toledo's Woolson Spice Company donated 14,000 pounds of coffee. The parade started at 10:30 a.m. The huge column proceeded west on Madison Avenue to Woodruff Avenue, then to Collingwood Boulevard, and south one block to Jefferson Avenue. The route turned east on Jefferson Avenue for an 18-block easterly trek back downtown. Toledo's veterans of the Forsyth Post were given the honor of being one of the leading units. Here they are beginning the grand parade on Madison Avenue.

As the marchers swung onto Jefferson Avenue, they were greeted by the "Living Flag." The official report of the Citizens' Committee described the flag as follows: "The grandstand for the 2,500 school children was erected on the little park facing Jefferson Avenue, where the old veterans on parade had a splendid view of it…The children were arranged on this stand in the national colors—the girls in red and white blouses forming the stripes, and the boys in blue and white shirts displaying the field of blue and the stars. Simply looked at as a picture it was inspiring and beautiful…But when the 2,500 voices were raised in song, assisted as they were by players on brass instruments, the volume of sweet sound and the beautiful scene were ravishing to the senses and uplifting to the soul. Our citizens will probably never again see a similar sight."* The students gave a stirring performance of patriotic songs, and spectators were amazed that the flag "waved with the regularity of the billows of the sea."* Many of the marching veterans were moved to tears by the sight and sound of the "Living Flag."

* Grand Army of the Republic. National Encampment. (42d:1908 Toledo, Ohio).Citizens' Committee. *Official souvenir forty-second National Encampment, Grand Army of the Republic August thirty-first to September fifth, Toledo, Ohio, 1908,* (Toledo, Ohio: The Franklin Printing & Engraving Co., 1908), 36.

PARADE ON JEFFERSON

From the "Living Flag," the grand procession continued into downtown on Jefferson Avenue. This overview photograph of the parade was taken from the roof of Milner's Department Store. The column is just reaching St. Clair Street and swinging left back toward Madison Avenue. The brand-new Secor Hotel—opened just in time for the Encampment—is seen in the background at the left.

BATTLE FLAGS

Obviously Ohio units were the most numerous participants in the GAR Encampment. The Ohio State Legislature had passed a resolution allowing the revered battle flags of the Ohio regiments to travel to Toledo from their place in the State Capitol. They were to be displayed at the Encampment and carried in the grand parade by representatives of each of their units. Because of the fragile condition of many of the banners, they were carried furled to avoid further damage.

The Wamba Carnival
Toledo's Mardi Gras of the North

TOLEDO BLADE DAILY WEEKLY

A snapshot of Mr. Taft taken in a lull of the G. A. R. Parade, Toledo, O., Sept. 2, '08.
COPYRIGHT APPLIED FOR

TAFT AND *THE TOLEDO BLADE*

William Howard Taft, soon to be elected the 27th President of the United States, was vacationing on Put-in-Bay. Taft was invited to be on the reviewing stand at Madison Avenue and 13th Street with other dignitaries including Ohio's governor and both Ohio senators. This photograph of Mr. Taft reading The Toledo Blade was taken by The Toledo Blade and published on a postcard. The remainder of the week was devoted to meetings and reunions known as "campfires" of individual units. The executive director of the Citizens' Committee recapped by proclaiming: "This vanishing army came to us, and with them the greatest multitude of people ever gathered in the Metropolis of the Maumee River." It was perhaps the city's finest hour in the national spotlight.

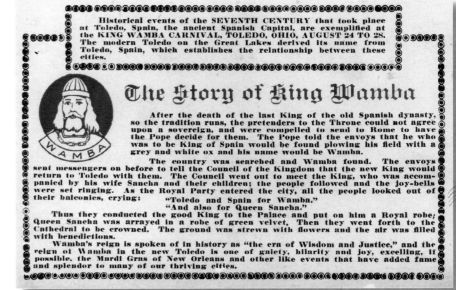

THE STORY OF KING WAMBA

The Grand Army of the Republic Encampment was a remarkable success and it gave Toledo national exposure. Local civic and business leaders were so impressed that further ideas to promote Toledo and its commercial advantages were immediately proposed. Enthusiasm combined with civic pride was so great that plans for another major event were formulated within 15 days of GAR week. The Toledo Commerce Club* announced a week-long carnival, patterned after New Orleans' Mardi Gras, for the following summer. Because Toledo's namesake+ is a city in Spain, it was decided to follow a Spanish theme, incorporating the story of the mythical miracle-performing, seventh-century Spanish King Wamba and his wife, Queen Sancha. The legend is printed on the accompanying postcard.

---

* The Toledo Commerce Club has evolved into today's Toledo Regional Chamber of Commerce.
+ No one knows who suggested the name Toledo for the new town resulting from the merger of Port Lawrence and Vistula. Most historians agree that the name was taken from Toledo, Spain. Judge John Killits, who published *Toledo and Lucas County Ohio* in 1923; H.S. Knapp, author of *History of the Maumee Valley*, published in 1877; and Charles S. Van Tassel, who's *Story of the Maumee Valley* appeared in 1929, all credit Willard J. Daniels. Daniels, a merchant in Vistula who had just purchased property in Port Lawrence, had been reading Spanish history and offered the name of the Spanish capital. He proposed that Toledo was easy to pronounce, had a pleasant sound, and was not being used by any other city in the United States.

WAMBA ANNOUNCEMENT

A planning committee of prominent businessmen headed by Adelbert L. Spitzer studied festivals in other cities. Planning for Toledo's great carnival continued for the entire year. Unlike the GAR Encampment, there was to be nothing solemn about the carnival. Mayor Brand Whitlock expressed his belief that the whole project was frivolous and designed mainly to relieve people of their money. Since it was being organized by members of Toledo's high society, it is not surprising that many of the events were targeted for the wealthy. Later this aristocratic focus was criticized as one of the reasons the Wamba Carnival was never repeated. Promotional items were distributed in Toledo and in communities within a 150-mile radius. These included news releases, posters, and postcards such as the one shown here.

SPANISH GUEST

The organizers of the Wamba Carnival invited King Alphonso XIII of Spain. The king agreed to send his diplomatic minister for the event. The Marquis de Villalobar is pictured in this postcard riding with W. L. Milner, president of The Toledo Commerce Club.

WAMBA DECORATIONS

Downtown was decorated for the Wamba Carnival as this spectacular view of Madison Avenue attests. Many merchants were able to reuse flags, bunting, and other decorations from the prior year's GAR Encampment.

WAMBA PLAZA

The center of activity for the carnival was a plaza created on Spielbusch Avenue. The street was blocked for construction of a midway containing all sorts of sideshow booths, animal acts, games of chance, flea circuses, and other amusements. Several local businesses displayed their products. An electrically-lighted triumphal arch welcomed visitors at the entrance to the plaza. The arch was made of wood covered with plaster of paris and featured a statue of King Wamba with two heralds on top. The plaza was officially opened with trumpet fanfare to kick off the carnival on Monday, August 23. The plaza remained open all week and attracted thousands of visitors.

THE ROYAL PAIR

The centerpiece event of the festival was the coronation of King Wamba and Queen Sancha on Tuesday, August 24. Adelbert L. Spitzer and a few members of the organizing committee chose secretly the couple to portray the king and queen from prominent Toledo families. The king was Robert Hixon, president of Hixon Lumber Company. The queen was teenage beauty Ethel Chesbrough, daughter of Aaron Chesbrough, the president of the Atwood Automobile Company. Attendants for the royal court were also selected from the top echelon of Toledo society. The king and queen made their grand appearance via the Maumee River on a "Royal Barge"—actually the decorated yacht of Commodore Solon O. Richardson of the Toledo Yacht Club. The barge embarked from the club on Maumee Bay and landed at the foot of Madison Avenue. The pair was greeted by trumpets and a contingent of attendants in costume. They ascended to Summit Street on a red carpet and entered a canopy-covered royal chariot pulled by six matching horses.

THE CORONATION

The entourage proceeded west on Madison Avenue to the triangle-shaped grove formed by 23rd Street, Jefferson Avenue, and Collingwood Boulevard. The king and queen climbed the stairs to the platform and the elaborate coronation ceremony ensued.

WELCOME BY MAYOR WHITLOCK

Following the crowning, Mayor Brand Whitlock gave a welcoming address. In this postcard view, the mayor—in the dark suit, center left, facing the royal couple seated on their thrones—is about to present the king and queen with the key to the city.

PRIZE WINNER

The rest of the week was filled with festivities and celebrations. Wednesday offered a day-long social gathering with music and picnicking at Walbridge Park. A parade in the evening featured more than one hundred elaborately-decorated vehicles. The presence of so many automobiles created significant interest as they were quite rare in 1909. The automobiles in the Wamba parade were decorated with canopies, flowers, and papier-mâché models of buildings and mountains. One was a Japanese garden covered with greenery and hanging lanterns. Another—that provoked much laughter from the onlookers—was topped with a caged "Wild Man from Borneo," wearing a necklace made of chicken feet and surrounded by barking dogs. A prize was awarded for the most beautiful entry. The winner, shown here, was an automobile decorated as a giant yellow butterfly with flapping wings and illuminated by tiny lights.

WAMBA CARNIVAL PARADE

Thursday, August 26, was the busiest day of the Wamba Carnival. Many businesses and factories in nearby towns closed on that day to allow workers to attend the festivities. Railroads, steamboat lines, and interurbans offered special excursions into Toledo. More than 100,000 visitors made the single day attendance the biggest gathering in the city's history. The highlight for most was the civic and industrial parade. Many local organizations, companies, and institutions participated—including all the city's uniformed divisions and every military and fraternal organization in town.

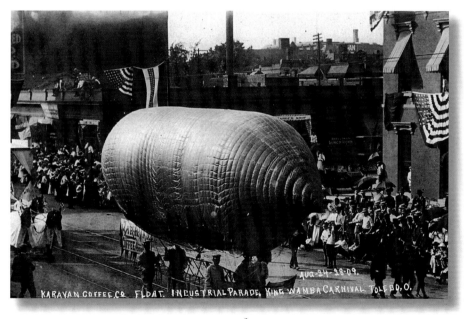

KNABENSHUE'S AIRSHIP

The Karavan Coffee Company enlisted Toledo's famous pioneer aviator, Roy Knabenshue, to provide an eye-catching promotion.

DOUBLE DECKER

Major Toledo businesses—including the Bell Telephone Company, the Gendron Wheel Company, and Toledo Scale—participated with floats. Shown here, the Milburn Wagon Works double-decked float features a patriotic theme.

LASALLE AND KOCH FLOAT

All the major retail stores also participated in the Wamba Carnival parade. One of the most elaborate and ornate floats was presented by the Lasalle and Koch Company.

Festivities continued throughout the week. On a spectacular "Venetian Night," hundreds of decorated boats and yachts created a lavish display. The concluding event of Wamba Week was a wild "Callithumpian Day"[1] carnival. Patterned after Fat Tuesday in New Orleans, masked and costumed members of the Traveling Men's Association and other businessmen rode papier-mâché horses through the streets amid general revelry. The greatest party in Toledo's history was considered a success, at least economically. Visitors spent large amounts of money with the Toledo merchants at the carnival. The event—as a form of modern civic advertising—also helped promote Toledo to the outside world.

1. A callithump is a noisy boisterous band or parade.

Jack Dempsey versus Jess Willard
World's Heavyweight Championship
Boxing Match

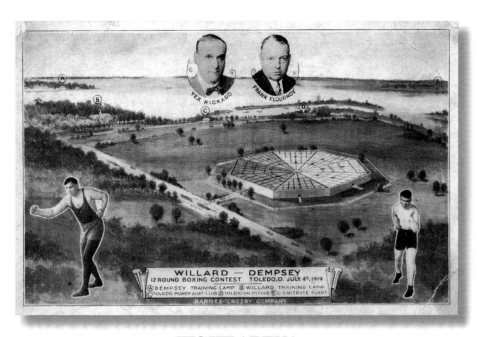

FIGHT ARENA

Toledo hosted one of the greatest sporting events of the twentieth century—the world's heavyweight championship boxing match on July 4, 1919. Reigning champion Jess Willard and challenger Jack Dempsey were the combatants for the scheduled 12-round bout.

The fight came to Toledo thanks to a deal made by Addison Q. Thacher, a member of the Toledo Boxing Commission, manager of the Toledo Athletic Club, and local politician.* Thacher took advantage of boxing promoter Tex Rickard's difficulty in finding a venue that would accept the bout. Thacher convinced Rickard that Toledo's crossroads location would make access convenient for out-of-town spectators. He assured the promoter that if he paid seven percent of the fight's proceeds to Mayor Cornell Schreiber's charity fund, there would be no political difficulties. Rickard agreed and paid $100,000 to build a primitive 80,000-seat stadium at Bay View Park. He advertised the upcoming Toledo spectacle all over the country.

* Addison Q. Thacher served as mayor of Toledo from January 1932 to December 1933.

Courtesy of Mark Walczak.

JESS WILLARD

Jess Willard was a giant of a man—six feet, six inches tall and 250 pounds. Despite a non-aggressive personality and embarking on a boxing career later in life, his great size and endurance carried him to the championship. He gained the title in a grueling 26-round bout against out-of-shape and over-the-hill black American expatriate Jack Johnson in Cuba in 1915. Willard had not fought since then, but agreed to defend his title simply because of the amount of money involved. This postcard photo was taken at Willard's training facility in Toledo. The big man is posing with his manager and two of his sparring partners.

JACK DEMPSEY

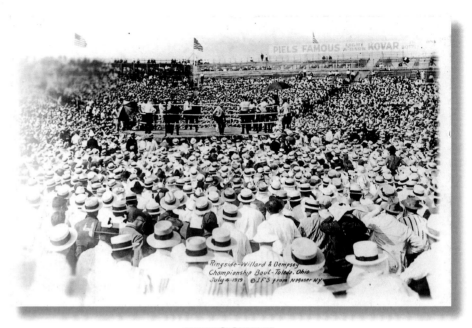

RINGSIDE

At age 24 Jack Dempsey was 12 years younger than Willard, but at six feet tall and 187 pounds, he gave six inches and nearly 60 pounds to his opponent. However, Dempsey was more aggressive and much faster than the champion. It was said he could snatch flies off the wall with two fingers and read the label on a spinning phonograph record. Dempsey, who was part Irish, Scottish, and American Indian, started boxing in 1911 at age 16. He had knocked out 42 opponents and defeated all the heavyweight contenders that Tex Rickard had hoped would challenge Willard. In 1917 Dempsey retained the aggressive and sometimes unscrupulous Jack "Doc" Kearns as his manager. Rickard was skeptical as he thought that Dempsey was too small to challenge Willard. Kearns was able to convince him otherwise, and secured a contract for Dempsey that paid $25,000 plus $2,500 expenses.

On the day of the fight, Independence Day 1919, the temperature in Toledo reached 95 degrees. Security was enforced at the entrance gate by two legendary, but aging lawmen, Bat Masterson and Wyatt Earp. The pair confiscated any guns brought to the arena by spectators. The crowd inside was a sea of straw hats and short-sleeved white shirts, estimated to be a disappointing number of less than 20,000. One problem for the spectators was that green lumber was used to construct the bleachers. Pine sap oozed in the extreme heat, making it impossible to sit without ruining one's clothes. Vendors quickly sold out of their supplies of ten-cent cushions. Concession rights had all been sold to local merchants, but the extreme heat ruined much of the food and melted the ice cream. Sales of lemonade, which should have been brisk, fell off drastically when a rumor spread among the crowd that someone had taken a bath in a barrel of it that morning. Whether true or not, the beneficiaries of the tale were a group of enterprising young boys who carried buckets of cool water around and sold it to the spectators at fifty cents per common dipper.

PRE-FIGHT INSTRUCTIONS

Dempsey later said, "Willard and I were called to the center of the ring for pictures." This postcard is one of those pictures. Toledoan Ollie Pecord, a member of the Toledo Boxing Commission and a former Toledo professional baseball player, was appointed referee for the bout. He is standing between the two fighters, wearing the beret.*

* Jack Dempsey with Barbara Piatelli Dempsey. The Destruction of a Giant: How I Beat Jess Willard, (*American Heritage Magazine*, vol. 28, April 1977), 72.

FIGHT ACTION

For about 30 seconds after the opening bell, the two combatants circled and sized each other up. Then, suddenly, Dempsey unleashed a crushing left hook to the side of Willard's face, and the champion went down. He scrambled to his feet, but was already groggy. The blow had broken his cheekbone in several places and knocked out at least one of his teeth. For the rest of the round Dempsey battered Willard all over the ring, knocking him down seven times.

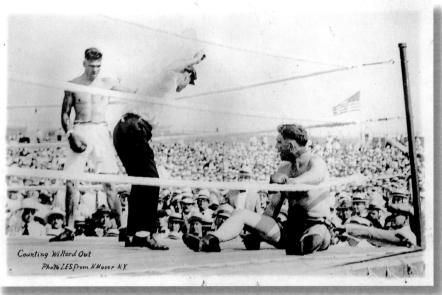

COUNTING WILLARD OUT

After the seventh knockdown, Willard was unable to get up and referee Pecord counted him out. Dempsey's manager, "Doc" Kearns, was beside himself with joy as he had placed a ten-thousand-dollar bet at ten-to-one odds with a local gambler. The bet was made "on behalf of a friend" and stipulated that Dempsey would knock out Willard in the first round. With visions of $100,000 dancing in his head, Kearns rushed Dempsey out of the ring and toward the dressing room. However—and unfortunately for Willard—the champion had been saved by the bell, which had rung, unheard in the crowd noise, at the count of seven. Dempsey was hustled back into the ring to avoid being disqualified—returning just in time for the start of the second round.

HEAVY PUNISHMENT

By sheer determination Willard was able to hold on for two more rounds, absorbing a terrific beating. Dempsey later admitted he felt sick at the sight of his battered and bloodied opponent and was shocked at how much damage he had inflicted. Willard could not continue and did not come out for the fourth round, making Jack Dempsey the new heavyweight champion. This postcard view shows the pummeled Willard under siege during the last round. It was later used by artist James Montgomery Flagg as the basis for a large oil painting. Romanticized, the work captured the spirit of Dempsey's victory. The painting is now at the Museum of American Art in Washington, D.C. For many years it hung in the restaurant operated by Dempsey in New York City. Dempsey would often greet his customers and ask where they lived. If the answer was Toledo, his response would invariably be that he had never heard of it. Afterwards he would often sit and have a drink with his Toledo fans. Because of Dempsey's fight with Jess Willard, many people all over the country now knew about Toledo.

CHAPTER TEN
A POSTCARD MEDLEY

During the period of Toledo's transformation into a modern urban metropolis, momentous events were recorded on postcards. Postcards were not designed to be a historical record, but from our perspective today, that is exactly what they are. We enjoy the unintended benefit—the preservation of earlier times.

This final chapter presents a few examples of the types of developments and events that Toledoans considered important during the city's early years. Many other subjects could have been chosen, but the compilers hope these examples will serve as an incentive to explore the accompanying digital archive of nearly 2,000 postcards—each with its own unique story to tell.

John Gunckel
and the Toledo Newsboys

Joe E. Brown was a Toledo newsboy who became a successful actor and comedian. Born in Holgate, Ohio, he moved to Toledo as a young child. He was a newsboy before joining the circus at age ten. In his biography, *Laughter is a Wonderful Thing*, he describes what it was like being a newsboy in Toledo circa 1900. He wrote: "I was seven when I finally persuaded Mother I should help support the family… In those days a boy could buy one of the Toledo papers (the Bee) for half a cent and sell them for one cent each. I had seen other boys run along the street in the evening yelling the news. It looked like a wonderful opportunity to make money. I could run and I could yell, as fast and as loud as the next. Mother…gave me a nickel…Five cents bought ten papers which gave me a profit of five cents—if I sold all the papers. I hurried to the alley back of the Toledo Bee on St. Clair Street. Already there was a line of about fifteen kids waiting for papers. Seniority or fists (or both) determined a kid's position in that line…For all my yelling and frantic running, I sold only four papers. I was stuck with six, or a net loss of one cent…Then came the big day when I sold all my papers…That night

I came home with a profit of eight cents. It was a proud moment when I walked in and handed Mother a nickel and three pennies. 'My little Businessman,' she called me. It was the greatest moment of my life up to that time."[1]

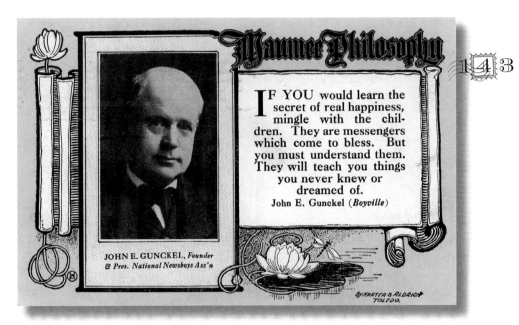

JOHN GUNCKEL, FOUNDER

In 1892 John Elstner Gunckel, Toledo businessman and agent for the Lake Shore and Michigan Southern Railroad, befriended and organized a number of unruly Toledo newspaper boys into a beneficial affiliation—The Toledo Newsboys' Association. It was the first organization of its type in the country. The mission of the association was to help young boys grow into respectable citizens. The boys were permitted to help govern and police themselves under a strict code of moral behavior. The Newsboys' basic guidelines included no swearing, no stealing, no gambling, no smoking, and no drinking. Punishment for violating these rules was forfeiture of membership in the organization. Membership grew and benefited hundreds of Toledoans over many years. The Toledo Newsboys' Association helped mold numerous successful leaders of the city.

1. Joe E. Brown. *Laughter is a Wonderful Thing*, (New York: A.S. Barnes & Company, 1956), 10-11.

GUSTAV KOEHLER

Gustav Koehler was an inexhaustible music teacher and band director who groomed the Newsboys' Band into a top-notch organization. Koehler is credited with teaching more than one thousand Toledoans to play band instruments during his long career. He structured and directed the Toledo Newsboys' Band, the Willys-Overland Band, the Toledo Police Band, the International Order Odd Fellows Band, the Toledo Military Band, the City Silver Coronet Band, and the Post Office Band. At one time he had nine musical groups under his tutelage. In the early 1900s his orchestra played for many local society gatherings.

Toledo Newsboys' Band, Toledo, Ohio

NEWSBOYS' BAND

The Toledo Newsboys' Association grew rapidly and developed many social and educational programs. The group formed a 38-piece band and a drill team of cadets. Local businesses and news media supported the Newsboys by purchasing instruments and uniforms. The band and drill team participated in parades and other civic functions.

MARCHING NEWSBOYS

The Toledo Newsboys' Band became highly skilled and was an appreciated participant in important events, including the GAR Encampment and the Wamba Carnival shown here.

Toledo Newsboys Cadets, Co. A, at St. Louis, 1904

NEWSBOYS AT WORLD'S FAIR

John Gunckel addressed the meeting of the National Association of Managers of Newspaper Circulation at the St. Louis World's Fair in the summer of 1904. He spoke to them about the benefits of his organization for boys. He emphasized that a better boy does a better job, which would increase circulation and profits. His ideas, and the Toledo example, became the basis for the formation of the National Newsboys' Association, benefiting children all over the country. Gunckel was named the first president of the national body. The performance of the Toledo cadets at St. Louis impressed the newspapermen and helped promote the idea of a national association. The Toledo Newsboys' Association became so well-known that the following year President Theodore Roosevelt invited 65 of its band members and cadets to Washington, D.C. to participate in his inauguration festivities.

2025-NEWSBOY'S PARADE, TOLEDO, OHIO.

NEWSBOYS ON PARADE

John Gunckel eventually earned the support of many Toledo businesses. Because of their contributions of money, goods, and clothing, many poor Newsboys and their families were helped. In 1908 he raised $100,000 from these supporters to erect a Newsboys' Building to provide a place for boys to gather for fellowship. On April 11, 1908, a parade featuring the Newsboys' Band was held that drew attention to the upcoming groundbreaking for the building. Located at Superior and Orange streets, the building was dedicated in 1911 and became a model for future institutions.

NEWSBOYS' MILESTONE

On April 11, 1908, Mayor Brand Whitlock, hat in hand, addressed the crowd and congratulated Mr. Gunckel, wearing the bowler hat, at the groundbreaking for the Toledo Newsboys' Association Building.

NEWSBOYS' BUILDING

The Newsboys' Building contained a 1,100-seat auditorium, a gymnasium, a swimming pool, and other recreational and educational facilities. A library encouraged members to read and prepare themselves for success in life. The administrative offices for the organization were also located at the site. The Toledo Newsboys' Association officially became the Boys Club of Toledo in 1942. In 1985 the organization was renamed the Boys & Girls Club of Toledo.

CUB LION, AGE 8 MONTHS, CHRISTENED "GUNCK" ON ANNUAL ZOO DAY
OF THE TOLEDO ZOOLOGICAL SOCIETY, MAY 8TH, 1915

GUNCK

John Gunckel made a significant contribution to America's social life. He was truly revered in Toledo and known affectionately to the boys as "Gunck." This eight-month-old lion cub was christened "Gunck" at the annual zoo day in 1915. When Gunckel died, more than 1,500 Newsboys came to pay their last respects at his funeral. Each brought a stone that was used to create a unique monument in the shape of a pyramid at his grave in Woodlawn Cemetery.

12655   UP THE MAUMEE FROM WALBRIDGE PARK, TOLEDO, OHIO.   COPR. DETROIT PUBLISHING CO.

City-owned Walbridge Park opened in 1888 and immediately became popular. It was set along the widest expanse of the Maumee River, two miles south of downtown.

THE PICNIC GROUNDS, WALBRIDGE PARK, TOLEDO, O.

PICNIC

Walbridge Park encompassed 69 riverfront acres. It was made easily accessible when a trolley line was extended out Broadway to its site. The setting and trees attracted crowds of picnickers and those who enjoyed taking strolls in the peaceful surroundings.

148

WALBRIDGE ENTRANCE

Visitors could roam among inviting flower beds at the park's entrance.

BOAT LANDING

*Walbridge Park's boat landing made boating and canoeing possible. Shown here,
a line of people wait for a ride on the Maumee River.*

OPITZ FOUNTAIN

Park patrons enjoyed the Opitz Fountain and the conservatory that was filled
with botanical curiosities. The fountain was made possible by a bequest of one thousand
dollars to Walbridge Park from the estate of Reinhold Opitz. He was an accountant in
Toledo and a member of the school board who enjoyed the park. The fountain was dedicated on July 12, 1905 as the Opitz Family Memorial. The Toledo Blade described
the fountain: "The drinking fountains will be novel, for there will be no cups. The dry
excursionists will insert their mouths into a constantly flowing font. There will be eight
streams, each one-fourth of an inch in diameter, to quench the thirst. The operation is
simple and requires no practice. Just aim the mouth at the stream, and it'll do the rest."
The upper portion was a seven-foot tall Grecian lady. She has been restored and stands
in the Formal Garden, formerly the Edna Ford Knight Memorial Garden*, at The
Toledo Zoo.

* The Edna Ford Knight Memorial Garden became the Formal Garden in 1972.

STEAMER ARAWANNA

Rowboats, sailboats, and canoes were available to rent from private boating concessionaire E.W. Ott. His steamer Arawanna, shown here, could be chartered for pleasure cruises.

THE TOLEDO ZOO

Beginning in the fall of 1900, visitors could enjoy The Toledo Zoo. The zoo began when a farmer gave an animal he claimed was a "young bear" to the Hildebrand brothers. The brothers in turn gave it to Milton L. Moore, Toledo's Superintendent of Parks, who built a cage for it at Walbridge Park.

Though represented as a bear, the Walbridge Park "Zoo's" initial specimen was a woodchuck. Nonetheless, the woodchuck attracted so much attention that officials decided a zoo would be a popular addition to the park. Two badgers and a golden eagle were donated. John Kuhlman, a patron, bought three real black bears from the Detroit Zoo to add to the menagerie.

JOSIE

A public subscription raised the money for the zoo to purchase the elephant Josie from the Ringling Brothers and Barnum & Bailey Circus in 1905.

After Josie died, another public subscription raised $2,000 to purchase the zoo's second elephant in 1912. The zoo claimed Babe was the largest elephant in North America.

Babe, Largest Elephant in Captivity   Toledo Zoological Gardens

BABE

THE MIDWAY, WALBRIDGE PARK, TOLEDO, O.

MIDWAY ON BROADWAY

Because of the immense popularity of Walbridge Park, private entrepreneurs began establishing businesses nearby. Buildings soon appeared along Broadway across from the park. The temptations depicted here include a confectionary advertising five-cent ice cream sodas, the Toledo Nickelodeon,* and a vaudeville theater.

* A nickelodeon is an early movie theater to which admission usually cost five cents—a nickel.

THE SCENIC

Prominent among the attractions on the Broadway midway near Walbridge Park was The Scenic amusement arcade shown here. Various enterprises came and went along the midway over the years. Among them were a figure-eight roller coaster, an elaborate carousel, a skating rink, bumper cars, a swan ride, and various food and beverage concessions. With all these activities complementing the beautiful Walbridge Park and the Maumee River, it is easy to understand why Walbridge Park was the most popular attraction in Toledo during the early decades of the twentieth century. Most of the midway was destroyed by fire in 1938, and the last of the remaining businesses closed in the late 1950s.

RIVER ICE

The Maumee River is a powerful force of nature. It can cause problems, particularly in late winter when ice and flooding can occur. From this February 19, 1908 postcard, it appears that ice could threaten the busy Cherry Street Bridge in the background.

NO.12. STEAMER YUMA LODGED IN CHERRY ST BRIDGE, 3-6-08. TOLEDO.O.

THE *YUMA* AND THE BRIDGE

On March 6, 1908, shortly after noon, the ice and high water tore the steel steamer Yuma away from her mooring at the foot of Madison Avenue. The current pushed the helpless vessel downriver until it crashed into the far west span of the Cherry Street Bridge. Toledo's harbormaster, John A. Page, was on the bridge at the moment of impact and was thrown into the river. He was unhurt and quickly rescued. Not so fortunate was Stephen Caswell, an East Side resident. He was struck in the head by the flying hawser used to secure the Yuma as it snapped from the piling around which it had been fastened. He was taken to the hospital where he died before his wife could reach him. She was delayed because the bridge was impassable.

Just before the span fell into the river

DISTRESSED BRIDGE

The impact of the Yuma striking the Cherry Street Bridge was so great that it moved that section of the bridge off its piers. This postcard shows that the trolley tracks were bent by the force of the collision.

Two-and-a-half hours after the collision, the entire west span of the bridge collapsed and fell into the river. Hundreds of spectators came to watch the tragedy unfold. The Toledo Blade printed an extra edition that afternoon giving complete details under the headline: "CHERRY ST. BRIDGE GOES DOWN."

NO.69. CHERRY ST BRIDGE SHOWING SPAN GONE, & THE YUMA. 3-6-08. TOLEDO.O

FALLEN SPAN

TEMPORARY SPAN

The loss of the bridge was a serious problem. It severed the main access road and the electric lines between the East Side and downtown. Since Toledo's only electricity-generating plant was on the west side of the river, the 25,000 residents of the East Side were also without electricity. The city rushed to build a temporary wooden span to close the gap. This postcard view shows the temporary span. Trolley tracks and electric power lines also were restored.

Cherry Street. New Million Dollar Bridge, commenced in 1910. To be completed in 1914. One side to be opened April 1st.

THE NEW CHERRY STREET BRIDGE

The accident forced the city to build a new Cherry Street Bridge. As this rendering illustrates, the new bridge is under construction while the older one behind it is still in use. The publisher of the postcard apologizes for the way the old bridge "rather spoils the view" of the exciting one being built. The new Cherry Street Bridge was completed in late 1913.

Opening Day at Swayne Field
July 3, 1909

Courtesy of Gary Gatanis.

LANDMARK IN THE MAKING

OPENING CEREMONY

Swayne Field was the brainchild of Toledoan Noah Swayne and Mud Hens President William Armour. Swayne provided the land at the northwest corner of Monroe Street and Detroit Avenue. Armour supplied the capital, or so it was believed at the time. Armour represented himself as the Mud Hens owner, but it was later learned that he was the front man for Charles Somers, owner of the Cleveland American League team. The pair's plans for Swayne Field were first announced in The Toledo Blade *on January 25, 1909 and construction began on March 6. The project was a huge undertaking with an ambitious schedule. The grandstands and bleachers, club houses, ticket offices, a concrete fence, and the playing field itself were to be ready for play on July 3, 1909. The grandstands were constructed of steel and reinforced concrete, and were said to be fireproof. The facilities rivaled those of Philadelphia's Shibe Park, the major league's first concrete and steel arena that also opened in 1909. This postcard photograph reveals the progress that had been made by April 25.*

Opening day was all that was promised. The press had been touting the event for weeks. The opening was timed so that arch rival Columbus would be in town. Armour had given up his field managerial duties for 1909 in order to concentrate on finances, construction, and, most importantly, purchasing the players who would bring Toledo a championship team. He had promised that there would be no finer team in the American Association, but by the season's halfway point that was not the case—Toledo was in last place. Mayor Brand Whitlock delivered the dedication address at the opening ceremony. He is shown here with his Columbus counterpart, Mayor Charles Anson Bond.

TOLEDO & COLUMBUS HAVE HOISTED THE FLAG

FLAG RAISING

Both teams participated in the flag-raising ceremony at the pole located in center-field. The outfield expanse was vast—the largest playing surface in the country. The fence, as shown in this postcard photograph, was an innovative design and the only one in the country made of concrete. It was twelve-feet high, and President Armour promised to have it decked with vines and flowers "to add to the beauty of the neighborhood." However, The Toledo Blade identified its true purpose: "It will be tough on the small boys, for it will be almost proof against climbing over, and no knives will penetrate it." The left field portion of the wall still stands.

NO. 26 WILLYS-OVERLAND EMPLOYEES STARTING FOR SWAYNE FIELD ON OPENING DAY, TOLEDO, OHIO.

OPENING DAY

Opening day at Swayne Field was for the fans, and 9,350 of them attended the inaugural game. Factories and businesses shut down to allow workers to attend the ball game. In this postcard, employees at Willys-Overland are assembled and ready to march to Swayne Field. The 1,000 upper deck grandstand seats were available at one dollar each, 1,596 lower grandstand seats at 75 cents each, another 3,304 at 50 cents each, and 6,000 bleacher seats at 25 cents each. The crowd was the largest in Toledo baseball history, but not every seat was filled.

THE GAME

The first game at Swayne Field was one of the most exciting on record, but the Mud Hens came out on the short end of a 12-11 score after 18 innings. The "double" contest was played in 3 hours and 35 minutes. Swayne Field went on to live a long life. During its existence, it continued to be the home of professional baseball, including Negro League baseball, and showcased other events as well. Amateur baseball, Major League exhibition games, football, golf demonstrations, automobile daredevil shows, dog races, and beauty pageants were presented over the years. Swayne Field was razed to make room for a shopping center following the 1955 season.

THE BILLY SUNDAY SMILE

William Ashley "Billy" Sunday, Sr. was a popular major league baseball player in the 1880s. He left baseball for the Christian ministry and became the nation's most famous evangelist during the first two decades of the twentieth century. He conducted Billy Sunday Evangelistic Meetings featuring his energetic preaching in large cities all over America. It is said that he preached the gospel to more people than any other person had until his time. Billy Sunday brought his "smile that won't come off" to Toledo in 1911.

TABERNACLE CONSTRUCTION

Billy Sunday held six weeks of revival meetings in downtown Toledo. A tabernacle was erected on the site of Armory Park on Spielbusch Avenue. This postcard view, taken on March 20, 1911, shows volunteers helping the contractors to finish the building.

BILLY SUNDAY ARRIVES

Sunday arrived by interurban car on April 8, 1911, and was greeted by a large welcoming committee of his Toledo delegates. The Sunday organization had established the Toledo Evangelistic Association well in advance of his visit to provide support for his meetings. The group was headed by local clergy and business leaders.

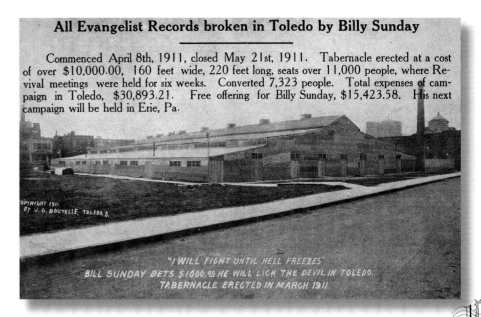

SUNDAY IN TOLEDO

For six weeks Billy Sunday held revival meetings at the tabernacle, declaring: "I will fight till hell freezes" and betting one thousand dollars that he would "lick the devil in Toledo." Three revival meetings were held daily, except on Mondays. At the final service on May 21, there were 341 conversions—a record service for Billy Sunday. The statistics for the Toledo campaign are printed on the front of this card.

While in Toledo, Sunday gave the funeral sermon for Addie Joss. Joss was a former Mud Hen pitching great who was at the top of his Hall of Fame career with the Clevelands* of the American League when he died of tubercular meningitis at age 31. Never had a player of such stature died while still in the game. Joss had made his home in Toledo since winning 44 games for the Mud Hens during the 1900 and 1901 seasons and was a very popular figure in the city. His funeral was the largest in Toledo since the Mayor "Golden Rule" Jones rites in 1904. More than 5,000 people came to pay their respects. It was attended by Cy Young and the entire Cleveland club along with Ty Cobb and the Detroit team. A local report said of the crowd: "All classes and kinds of men, women and children were represented in that throng. That Addie was a universal favorite everyone knew, but no one realized the general sadness that would be manifested at his death."+

Sunday returned to Toledo on September 4, 1911, for a picnic with the converts from his spring campaign.

* Before nicknames became commonplace, baseball teams were known by their city. The team from Cleveland, Ohio was the Clevelands. In this case, the Cleveland team was also called the Naps for their player-manager, Napoleon Lajoie.
+ This quotation is taken from an unidentified newspaper clipping written by Tom Terrell, April 17, 1911.

The Garden
of Eden

Doc Hettinger, The Man of Vision

THREE VISIONS

Toledo's Garden of Eden was created by optician and Pentecostal minister Cassius M. "Doc" Hettinger. Following three vision experiences, he began building the "garden" at his home at 1104 Upton Avenue in 1919. He decorated his house and yard and built a chapel out of thousands of shells he collected at Reno Beach. Marriages were performed in the chapel. His creation became a pilgrimage site for people from all over the world.

Some visitors treated the garden with reverence. However, many Toledoans tolerated the attraction with a mix of humor and embarrassment.

MAN OF VISION

Although Hettinger never admitted to charging admission, the Garden of Eden appeared to some to be a commercial enterprise. In 1951 neighbors appealed to the city to stop the intrusion into their neighborhood. They claimed that a nuisance was created when as many as 22 busloads of visitors toured the garden on a weekend. After some spirited debate, city council allowed the Garden of Eden to continue with the provision that Hettinger install public restrooms and lower a wall in accordance with existing city ordinances. Mr. Hettinger died in 1955, but his wife kept the garden open until circa 1965 when she finally closed it due to physical deterioration and declining interest. The home was demolished about 1970.

TOLEDO SHORTLY AFTER 1930

This postcard shows Toledo shortly after 1930—at the close of the Golden Age described in *You Will Do Better in Toledo*. This crowded downtown is a result of the growth the city experienced from about 1880 through 1930. During this half century, manufacturing transformed the city's economic base and the population increased nearly six-fold to 290,000 residents, commerce and opportunities for business exploded, and a grander physical plant gave Toledo a new downtown skyline and its own recognizable architectural signature. Toledoans created a distinctive mix of parks and a zoo, recreational and sports facilities, a top-of-the-line professional baseball park, indoor and outdoor entertainment venues and theaters, and cultural institutions including the foundation of what would become one of the finest art museums in the country.

The development of simplified and affordable photography coupled with the gift by United States Postal Service of inexpensive postage rates, made the penny picture postcard possible during this time frame. We are fortunate to have this pictorial documentation available for those years.

During a significant portion of this Golden Age, Toledo was one of the fastest-growing cities in the country. Most residents and outside observers optimistically believed the city would continue to grow and prosper at its former pace for decades into the future. It did not—in fact growth slowed substantially. Many factors drove Toledo off its course toward continued prosperity—its dependence on a few major industries, a number of damaging economic decisions in the 1920s, a disastrous worldwide depression, labor unrest and strikes, a Toledo banking crisis that almost bankrupted the city, a world war which only temporarily boosted the city's sagging economy, the decline of many of the old heavy industries, and growing global competition.

If Toledo expects to prosper in the years to come it must, once again, attract business and industry and develop a vibrant downtown. A century ago, business and industrial leaders built a robust and dynamic city—centered on an exciting downtown core that gave Toledo its characteristic identity. The city's future depends on rebuilding that core into a thriving center—this time featuring a modern urban landscape that will meet the needs of people and businesses in the years to come. The city center also will need to double as a regional center to benefit the entire area.

We are happy to present *You Will Do Better in Toledo*, and hope it will interest and enlighten many readers about the unique accomplishments of prior Toledoans. Our wish is that it will promote pride in our heritage and inspire the people of Northwest Ohio and Southeast Michigan to seek ways to improve our community so that we can once again proclaim to all we meet: "You Will Do Better in Toledo."

WE DID IT BEFORE—AND WE CAN DO IT AGAIN.

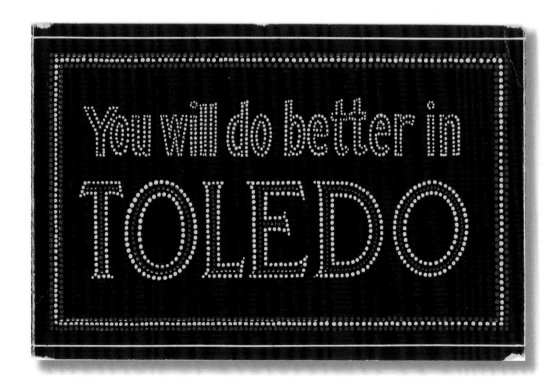

Books and Magazines

Brown, Joe E. *Laughter is a Wonderful Thing*, New York: A.S. Barnes & Company, 1956.

Butler, Frank E. *The Standby: An Autobiography*, F.E. Butler, 1990.

Dempsey, Jack with Barbara Piatelli Dempsey. The Destruction of a Giant: How I Beat Jess Willard, *American Heritage Magazine*, vol. 28, April 1977.

Downes, Randolph C. *Canal Days*, Toledo, Ohio: Historical Society of Northwestern Ohio, 1951.

————. *The Conquest*, Toledo, Ohio: Historical Society of Northwestern Ohio, 1948.

————. *Industrial Beginnings*, Toledo, Ohio: Historical Society of Northwestern Ohio, 1954.

————. *Lake Port*, Toledo, Ohio: Historical Society of Northwestern Ohio, 1951.

Fairfield, E. William. *Fire & Sand*, Cleveland: The Lezius-Hiles Company, 1960.

Glaab, Charles N. and Morgan J. Barclay. *Toledo: Gateway to the Great Lakes*, Tulsa, Oklahoma: Continental Heritage Press, Inc., 1982.

Grand Army of the Republic. National Encampment. (42d:1908 Toledo, Ohio).Citizens' Committee. *Official souvenir forty-second National Encampment, Grand Army of the Republic August thirty-first to September fifth, Toledo, Ohio, 1908*. Toledo, Ohio: The Franklin Printing & Engraving Co., 1908.

Gunckel, John E. *Boyville: A History Of Fifteen Years' Work Among Newsboys*, Toledo, Ohio: The Toledo Newsboys' Association, 1905.

Hage, Robyn and Larry Michaels. *A Chance for Every Child: History of Toledo Public Schools*, Toledo, Ohio: Bihl House Publishing, 2000.

Hartung, Walter H., Jr. *History of Medical Practice in Toledo and The Maumee Valley Area 1600-1990*, publisher unknown, 1992.

Husman, John R., ed. *Toledo: Our Life, Our Times, Our Town, Volume I*, Toledo, Ohio: The Blade, 2005.

Killets, John M. *Toledo and Lucas County, Ohio (3 vols.)*, Chicago: S. J. Clarke Company, 1923.

Knapp, H. S. (Horace S.). *History of the Maumee Valley*, publisher unknown, 1877.

Ligibel, Ted J. *The Toledo Zoo's First 100 Years: A Century of Adventure*, Virginia Beach, Virginia: The Donning Company/ Publishers, 1999.

Marshall, James C. *A Promise Kept: A History of the Village of Ottawa Hills*, Maumee, Ohio: Woodlands Publishing, 2003.

McMaster, Julie A. *The Enduring Legacy: A Pictorial History of the Toledo Museum of Art*, Toledo, Ohio: Toledo Museum of Art, 2001.

Michaels, Larry R. and Ronald J. Mauter. *East Toledo At Work: A History of Business and Industry of East Toledo*, Toledo, Ohio: Bihl House Publishing, 2006.

Mollenkopf, Jim. *Civil War Stories of Northwest Ohio Heroes*, Toledo, Ohio: Lake of the Cat Publishing, 2002.

Mollenkopf, Jim. *The Great Black Swamp: Historical Tales of Northwest Ohio*, Toledo, Ohio: Lake of the Cat Publishing, 1999.

Paquette, Jack. *The Glassmakers*, Toledo, Ohio: The Trumpeting Angel Press, 1994.

Porter, Tana Mosier. *Toledo Profile: A Sesquicentennial History*, Toledo, Ohio: Toledo Sesquicentennial Commission, 1987.

Revett, Marian S. *A Minstrel Town*, New York: Pageant Press, 1955.

Scott, Jesup Wakeman. *A Presentation of Causes Tending To Fit the Position of the Future Great City of the World in the Central Plain (2nd Revised Edition)*, Toledo, Ohio: Blade Printing Company, 1876.

Scribner, Harvey. *Memoirs of Lucas County and the City of Toledo (2 vols.)*, Madison, Wisconsin: Western Historical Association, 1910.

Skrabec, Quentin R. Jr. *Glass In Northwest Ohio*, Charleston, South Carolina: Arcadia Publishing, 2007.

Smith, R. Boyd, ed. *The Best of Smith's Cook Book and History*, publisher and date unknown.

Speck, William D. *Toledo: A History in Architecture 1835-1890*, Chicago: Arcadia Publishing, 2001.

———. *Toledo: A History in Architecture 1890-1914*, Chicago: Arcadia Publishing, 2002.

———. *Toledo: A History in Architecture 1914-Century's End*, Charleston, South Carolina: Arcadia Publishing, 2003.

Stevens, Nina Spalding. *A Man and a Dream: The Book of George W. Stevens*, Hollywood: Hollycrofters, circa. 1940.

Toledo Museum of Art. *Toledo Treasures: Selections From the Toledo Museum of Art*, New York: Hudson Hills Press, 1995.

University of Toledo, Urban Affairs Center, The. *Discover Downtown Toledo Walking Tour*, Toledo, Ohio: The University of Toledo, Urban Affairs Center, 2004.

Van Tassel, Charles Sumner. *Story of the Maumee Valley, Toledo, and the Sandusky Region*, Chicago: S. J. Clarke Publishing Company, 1929.

Waggoner, Clark. *History of the City of Toledo and Lucas County, Ohio*, Bowie, Maryland: Heritage Books, Inc., 1997 (reprint of Munsell & Co., New York, 1888).

Sources at the Toledo-Lucas County Public Library, Local History and Genealogy Department

Toledo history scrapbooks
Toledo city directories
Toledo Bee
The Toledo Blade
Toledo Commercial
Toledo News
Toledo News-Bee

Reference Works

The Chicago Manual of Style, 15th edition
Merriam-Webster's Collegiate Dictionary, tenth edition

Web Sites

ancestry.com
crm.cr.nps.gov
http://buckeyebeer20000.tripod.com
http://dictionary.reference.com
http://cweb2.loc.gov
www.bgctoledo.org
www.bgsu.edu
www.chicagopostcardmuseum.org
www.dominican.edu
www.emotioncards.com
www.findagrave.com
www.kodak.com
www.local12.org
www.measuringworth.com
www.memory.loc.gov
www.nysl.gov
www.ohiocenterforthebook.org
www.oldwestendtoledo.com
www.oplin.org
www.polishtoledo.com
www.searsarchives.com
www.toledosattic.org
www.vintagephoto.tv
www.wikipedia.org
www.willysoverland.com
www.wonderclub.com

INDEX

A NOTE ON THE TYPE

This book is composed of Horley Old Style, a typeface issued by the English type foundry Monotype in 1925. It has distinctive features such as lightly cupped serifs and an oblique horizontal bar on the lowercase "e."